BEYOND THE AMERICAN DREAM

Work and Wealth in the 21st Century

BEYOND THE AMERICAN DREAM

Work and Wealth in the 21st Century

by Thomas B. Carson

ISBN 1-58500-113-9

About the Book

At the millennium, many Americans are concerned about the future. To maintain contemporary lifestyles, many families require two incomes. Yet there is the dilemma of a decline in living standards in the face of robust economic growth. This book offers fresh insights into the fundamental, revolutionary changes occurring in the work force and the new creation of wealth. The author's optimistic view is that the scientific and technological revolutions currently underway may offer solutions to the very problems they create and pave the way for a renewal of the American dream.

**For Anne and
Nathalie**

One thing is certain. An innovation-led economy requires new policies and new politics.
Traditional liberal or conservative solutions to
problems based on an industrial-era paradigm
won't work. The real political split today in the
U.S. is between innovation optimists.... and
those who subscribe to a cramped view of the
economy's potential and the role the country
should play around the world.

Business Week
(August 31, 1998)

First Cybernetic Edition

TABLE OF CONTENTS

Chapter 1

Introduction: Visions of the Future of Work

Many observers of the American scene say everything is going well. The economy is unusually robust; inflation is relatively low and the unemployment rate is reaching record low levels. New jobs are being created, and the Federal budget is finally in the black for the first time since the sixties. Yet, at the same time, Americans feel a sense of unease. Corporate layoffs continue and many of the new jobs that are being created are in the low-salary range and without substantial retirement benefits, so that many families depend on two wage-earners to maintain their standard of living. Americans earning in the middle of the wage scale have seen their earnings decline since 1989, after adjustment for inflation, while the wages of those at either end have gained ground.[1] Across the race and economic spectrum, Americans worry about job stability for themselves and for their children in the future.

Jobs and job creation were major topics of the last Presidential campaign, and various remedies were offered but all seemed to ring hollow. There appears to be no national consensus on the cause of these events which, on the surface, seem to contradict each other. Why should the economy be growing when the job situation is so unclear? In the past, job losses went together with recessions or depression, not with a booming economy .

Many observers, including this writer, believe that the heart of the matter lies in what the economists call the structural—as opposed to cyclical, as in business cycles—nature of the changes occurring. A permanent and fundamental change is affecting not just the U.S. economy but other nations as well. A recent article in the high-tech magazine <u>Wired</u> sums up the situation nicely:

> … (T)he developed world is in the midst of a
> once-a-century paradigm shift: from the old in-
> dustrial order to the globally interdependent
> knowledge-based economy in ascendance. This

transformation is being wrought by chips and
bits [computers] and sparking minds, and the
vast bulk of it is affected by government only on
the margins.[2]

This change, which has been categorized as a "second industrial divide," a "post industrial economy" or a "Third Wave,"
is washing across the world like a powerful tide. It involves not
just the effects of computer and communications technologies
but a whole range of interrelated changes that have transformed
the economic context. We can now talk about a global economy
where workers all over the world are in direct competition with
each other for jobs, as nation-states lose control of their own
economies to impersonal market forces.

The brave new knowledge-based global economy which is
taking over from the former industrial one is truly something
new under the sun, causing a lot of head scratching as people
confront the necessity to rethink the old, familiar categories and
approaches to life (hence the term "paradigm shift," borrowed
from Thomas Kuhn's book on the nature of scientific revolutions).[3]

A number of social scientists have expressed widely differing opinions on the significance of these developments and their
relationship to future prospects for employment. They have offered varied, often contradictory, solutions for these problems.
Some see no problem and present a rosy scenario of jobs and
prosperity for all (or almost all) Americans. Others predict a
two-tiered society: the high-tech winners and all the rest (a vast
majority of the population) who will live in permanent poverty.

At the heart of the controversy is a general consensus on the
part of many that advanced technologies are bringing about a
fundamental and permanent change in the nature and availability
of work in the U.S. and other developed countries. A number of
observers, including this writer, are convinced that these technologies are not just changing the nature of work but, to some
extent, are permanently supplanting the need for human labor in
industries as well as in the so-called service sector, not only

2

among blue collar workers, but also in the ranks of management and even among highly-educated professionals. All this may lead to a strange anomaly: a highly productive economy —productivity being measured by volume of output per number of worker hours— which is run by a small number of knowledge workers, with the rest of the population unemployed or underemployed in the formal "productive" sense. Does this portend a permanent division of society into a small, wealthy, highly-educated, elite and a large mass of people sunk into ignorance and hopelessness, a situation one finds in many Third World countries and in literature (as was brilliantly portrayed in Kurt Vonnegut's 1958 science fiction novel, <u>The Player Piano)</u>?

Anyone who can provide the answer to this far-ranging question will have gone a long way toward solving what may well be a central dilemma facing American society as we enter the 21st Century. This book will not attempt such a Herculean task, but will offer some fresh insights into this perplexing matter, as well as some suggestions for further study and discussion. Most importantly, it is designed to familiarize the general reader with some of the major issues involving the future of work in the U.S. and other industrialized countries, as well as some of the public policy measures being discussed by the so-called "experts" in the field. The distinguished social scientist and management guru Peter Drucker has written: "(T)he disappearance of labor as a key factor of production is going to emerge as the critical unfinished business of capitalist society."[4] Another social scientist, Jeremy Rifkin, considers that redefining the role of the individual in a society absent of mass formal work is, perhaps, the seminal issue of the coming age.[5]

In recent years, a number of other specialists have studied this matter and, as might be expected, have widely differing views of the future, (some of which we will discuss in Chapters 2 and 3). Their policy prescriptions also vary and range from bleak pessimism, calling for extreme government measures, to heady optimism with a prescription for further reducing government intervention in people's lives. However, the experts generally share these convictions: the world is going through a major transition to a new era; this transition will be very rapid and far reaching; and one of the aspects of life which will be changed the most is the nature and availability of work in the U.S. and other developed countries.

In this writer's view, the best analyses of the problems created by the new advanced technologies belong to the pundits who view the future of the American economy with concern, although their policy recommendations are often marred by adherence to old socio-economic paradigms. The experts of an optimistic persuasion tend to grasp the great potential benefits of the new technologies but ignore or underestimate the social costs inherent in their implementation. This writer will attempt to strike a balance between these two schools of thought and try to reach a tentative synthesis of what appears to be two very different and contradictory approaches to the subject. In the next two chapters, I will briefly outline the opinions and policy recommendations of some leading "pessimists" and "optimists," as reflected in the writings of 17 experts, including Robert Reich, Harvard Professor and Secretary of Labor in Clinton's first administration; Thomas Donahue, former President of the AFL-CIO; Bill Gates of Microsoft; and Steve Forbes, President and CEO of Forbes, Inc.

Before attempting a synthesis of opinions on the future of work, I will introduce a subject which at first glance might appear to be a diversion from the main topic of this book but is actually an important element in considering the question of a "jobless future." This aspect of economic activity has arisen as an offshoot of the high-tech revolution and promises to have, on its own, a far-reaching effect on the political economy of nations. I refer to the evolution of a global money market, not controlled by any government or private agency, which has developed in the last 20 years or so. The purpose of introducing this new theme is twofold: first, to give a concrete example of the truly innovative role in human affairs played by advanced computer and communication technologies; second and more importantly, to make a point which has been often overlooked in policy discussions about the future of work: The increasing extent to which the global money market is becoming a co-partner with governments of so-called sovereign states in the over-all management of their economies. As one specialist in international finance recently put it:

> It is critically important for national governments to realize that the global capital market is now a powerful force of its own and that it will be progressively less possible for an individual government to pursue policies under the assumption that it can directly control its own domestic financial market. This will be true even of the largest nations, including the United States. This does not, however, mean that nations are powerless to influence their economies … [b]ut it does mean that governments will be less able to use their direct control of their domestic financial markets to achieve their [policy] objectives.

> Most people in each nation believe that their respective national governments still have complete control over their own local financial economy. In fact, they have lost much of their ability to control exchange rates or interest rates, and they are gradually losing control over the financial institutions they regulate.[6]

How is this trend in world financial markets relevant to the main theme of this book? The fact is that several of the major policy tools currently used by governments to stimulate their economies and create more employment opportunities are among those fiscal and monetary measures closely monitored by money markets, and these markets are beginning to have an appreciable measure of control—or at least veto power—over government policy. Thus, many of the more extreme policy recommendations which have been made to reduce unemployment brought about by the introduction of new technology may no longer be viable. Regardless of the wishes of a given government, the global capital market, which is rapidly gaining control of major world financial assets and owes allegiance to no country, can now—with respect to poorer countries and soon with respect to all countries—exercise indirect but extremely effective pressure on governments to avoid measures not favored by the market. In the case of the so-called developing countries, this pressure is direct and is usually exercised by such institutions as the World Bank and the International Monetary Fund (IMF).

This situation leads to a real dilemma: some highly esteemed experts believe that structural unemployment may become so pervasive in the U.S. and other countries that the only way to maintain social order is to adopt extreme fiscal and monetary measures to stimulate the economy and create, if necessary, public work programs of last resort along the lines of the Depression-era WPA. On the other hand, should these measures be introduced, they would probably be blocked by the global capital market and domestic opponents of such measures as being harmful to the credit-worthiness of the respective nations. The most powerful government tools to counteract growing unemployment caused by the technological revolution may no longer be fully available to policy makers.

Of course, there are those who argue that the situation is not as grim as depicted by some analysts and that—at least with respect to the U.S.—the resilient American economy can grow out of any such impasse, creating new jobs in areas of production not yet imagined by economists and other policy makers. These arguments are cold comfort to those who feel that every reasonable economic measure should be fully available for use in this uncertain and often frightening transition period.

At the same time, there is a new set of circumstances developing at a rapid pace which offers great promise for reaching solutions to the problem of joblessness facing the U.S. and other industrialized nations. These new circumstances which arise from the same scientific and technological advances mentioned above are often overlooked by many analysts of structural unemployment who tend to focus only on the negative effects of the high-tech revolution.

These new technologies offer an unprecedented potential for the creation of vast new sources of wealth, as well as new types of goods and services which can be used to solve some of the problems created by the same technologies. What is truly remarkable about these new technologies is their enormous and open-ended potential for wealth creation, far greater than anything the world has seen before. Dr. Carver Mead of The California Institute of Technology has written:

> (T)he entire Industrial Revolution … enhanced productivity by a factor of about a hundred, but the micro electronic revolution has already enhanced productivity in the information-based technology by a factor of more than one million, and the end isn't in sight yet.[7]

A leading international banker, Walter Wriston, agrees that

> …the world is changing not because computers have replaced clerk-typists and can produce more work in less time, but because the human struggle to survive and prosper now depends on an entirely new source of wealth [emphasis added]. It is information, knowledge applied to work to create value.[8]

Other far-sighted futurists such as Alvin Toffler (author of Future Shock and The Third Wave) and Peter Drucker share the concept that the revolution wrought by information technologies has created a major increase in the world's wealth through the exploitation of information, a resource that is not material in origin and, therefore, subject to depletion, but mental and, in theory, virtually inexhaustible.

Examples of how this new type of wealth will be brought about and advanced technologies which offer great potential for wealth creation will be discussed in Chapter 6. Two such principal technologies are biotechnology (the ability to manipulate life forms at the cellular and sub-cellular levels and thus create new types of plants and animals) and the new field just opening up which may offer the greatest potential for wealth creation in the next century: nanotechnology (the ability to manipulate <u>all matter</u> at an even more basic level—that of molecules and atoms).

These two technological fields can also be subsumed under the category of information technology since they, too, involve the application of information to create value, in this case, new or modified life forms and materials, the dream of the ancient alchemists. Other advanced technologies—such as high temperature superconductors, alternative energy sources including atomic fusion and new pharmaceuticals—offer great potential for increasing human wealth and welfare.

Many writers have pointed out the potential social and environmental risks and costs surrounding these new technologies, as well as the serious ethical problems they raise (e.g., the issue of human cloning). Without disparaging such views, I shall dwell on the positive aspects. A central tenet of this book is that the potential benefits to society of advanced technologies far outweigh the negative factors. These large potential increases in material abundance offer a possible way out of the policy dilemmas cited above, since vast increases in wealth could provide resources to alleviate some of the economic and social problems brought about by advanced technologies.

Any mention of vast new wealth raises the age-old issue of income redistribution and the capitalist system. Inequality of incomes inherent to capitalism is further aggravated by the effects of the information age economy which favors "knowledge" workers at the expense of others. Unless corrective measures are taken, this great potential wealth will accrue to only a small percentage of the population. Perhaps more important is the danger that the consumer base of the economy might be seriously eroded as the middle class is squeezed out; some observers believe this is already happening.

In the first decades of the next century we may be facing a defining moment in the history of the capitalist system. Will the owners and managers of capital rise to the occasion and realize that, altruism aside, their self-interest (to use a classic phrase) would lead them to accept additional income-sharing measures. Or will shortsightedness and greed prevail, leading to the sharply polarized, two-tiered society of haves and have-nots that some futurist writers project? In answer to this question I can only point out that some countries have a heritage of wealth-sharing and some do not. Up to the present, the U.S. has been in the former category and, hopefully, will remain so. Therefore, my view of the future is cautiously optimistic.

Another fundamental question: What kinds of jobs will be available in this brave new world? A number of books have been published on this subject recently, but not surprisingly, they are directed toward the "winners" in the future job market: the so-called knowledge-workers. Little attention is paid to those people who, for one reason or another, will not have the education and/or native talent and intelligence to enter the ranks of these privileged workers. Many futurists simply ignore these people, who will undoubtedly comprise the majority of the population. Among the few far-sighted writers who deal with this matter are management guru Peter Drucker, and economist and sociologist Hazel Henderson, who point out that work in the future will not be eliminated, but will have to be viewed and valued differently in an expanded context. In most countries, work is considered the central experience of adult life and a measure of self-worth, as well as an economic necessity. It is becoming increasingly clear that, thanks to advanced technologies, increasing numbers of workers are not needed in the formal "productive" economy. What, then, is the role, if any, of such persons in society? In many countries, the permanently unemployed find occupations in illegal activities such as the drug trade; others simply give up and become wards of the State. The writers believe that as jobs in the manufacturing and service sectors become automated, whole areas of work—previously ignored or undervalued in the market economy—will become attractive opportunities, although subsidies and other incentives may have to be offered to render them so. (We will discuss these concepts in Chapters 6 and 7, including some thoughts on the future role of labor unions.)

The "American Dream" is a term used to describe commonly-held beliefs, assumptions and expectations of political freedom, economic opportunity and material progress in the U.S. A number of contemporary writers have announced the decline and disappearance of the Dream, hastened by the forces of advanced technology. These jeremiads end on a note of pessimism, leading to the conclusion that only a planned society sharing austerity and hardship can weather these revolutionary changes.

I differ from this point of view and support the argument that such gloomy outcomes and anti-market solutions are not inevitable. Without endorsing the overly-optimistic predictions of such writers as Bill Gates and Newt Gingrich, I suggest that the scientific and technological revolutions currently underway may offer a solution to some of the dilemmas we are facing. In Chapter 8, I shall offer a positive vision of the future of work in this country and of the U.S. economy as a whole, based on the conviction that the same traditions of political freedom and economic and social openness to new ideas that helped to forge the American Dream will, despite all obstacles, provide us with the materials and will to refashion the Dream to meet the new conditions facing us in the years ahead.

Chapter 2

The Pessimists' Vision

As in so many instances involving predictions of things to come, there are two major and often opposing camps—the pessimists and the optimists—those who see the cup half empty and those who see it half full. The future of work in the U.S. is no exception. A leading analyst, Robert B. Reich, professor of political economy and Secretary of Labor in the first Clinton administration, has suggested that the situation is a bit more complicated:

> Conventional discussions of the economy—the gross national product, national economic growth, the nation's competitiveness—are beside the point, as are the predictable range of prognostications concerning the economy's future. The optimist's view is accurate—but only for a small portion of America's workers who are becoming ever more valuable in the world economy .... The pessimist's prognosis, on the other hand, is accurate for most other Americans, but it neglects this thriving minority, who represent one of the great successes of modern economic history. [1]

Reich's concern is that America is fast becoming what some observers call a two-tiered society. One group of workers, who have been dubbed the "knowledge workers," are the full beneficiaries of not just the global economy (a concept I will discuss in Chapter 4), but perhaps more importantly, the various technological and scientific advances which are bringing about a new era (often called the "Information Age," the "post-Industrial" or "Third Wave" society). I will discuss these privileged workers in the next chapter; this chapter is devoted to those who will benefit little or not at all from these major advances. Also, I will limit my discussion to the U.S. but, by extension, many workers in other industrialized countries, as well as legions of employed or jobless persons in the so-called Third World, fall into the category of those who will not immediately benefit from all the good things expected to come from the implementation of new advanced technologies.

Given the widespread unease about future prospects for a large number of the world's workers or would-be workers, the observers of a pessimistic bent have had a field day. A number of books and articles have come out recently predicting everything from a profound and continued economic downturn, to populist uprisings, a revival of statist solutions such as those used in Europe before World War II, and finally—on the radical Left—renewed predictions of social revolutions such as those which occurred in Russia and China earlier in this century.

To discuss all the analyses and prognostications of the pessimist's camp would require another book. I will attempt to give the reader a flavor of the arguments being put forth by leading writers who have focused on the negative effects on workers of the global economy and of technological advances, referring to some dozen books and articles that have appeared recently, and attempting a summary of their principal recommendations.

Robert Reich in The Work of Nations puts recent developments in the labor market in historical perspective by first tracing the rise of large industrial concerns in the U.S. These core corporations not only flooded America with goods but also created millions of jobs that swelled the ranks of America's middle class, and in turn enlarged the mass market for mass- produced goods. By the mid-1950s, almost half of all American families fell comfortably within this middle group. Notably, most of the middle-class families were headed not by professionals or business executives but by skilled and semi-skilled factory workers and clerks who managed the flows of product and paperwork through the great corporations. As Reich states: "The prosperity and growth of America's middle class was one of American capitalism's greatest triumphs for which the core American corporation can claim significant credit."[2]

American workers and their families benefited from both higher wages and increased social benefits negotiated by the labor unions which represented their interests. Reich points out that for more than a quarter century, from the end of World War II until 1973, the real wages of America's production workers grew, on average, 2.5 to 3 percent each year. Benefits grew in tandem. In 1950, only 10 percent of union contracts provided for pensions and only 30 percent included social insurance; five years later, 45 percent provided their workers with pensions and 70 percent offered life, accident and health insurance, including hospitalization and maternity care.[3]

Other benefits included paid vacations, supplemental unemployment payments for laid-off workers and wages which were automatically adjusted upward for cost of living increases brought on by inflation.

This situation, so ideal for American families in the immediate post-World War II period—a situation closely identified with the belief in the possibility of prosperity and upward mobility for all often called the "American Dream"—has radically changed. America's core corporations no longer plan and implement the production of a large volume of goods and services; they no longer own and invest in a vast array of factories, machinery, laboratories, warehouses, and other tangible assets; they no longer employ armies of production workers and middle-level managers; they no longer serve as a gateway to the American middle class. As Reich states, "The core corporation is no longer even American. It is, increasingly, a façade, behind which teems an array of decentralized groups and subgroups continuously contracting with similarly diffuse working units all over the world".[4]

This new type of business, which Reich calls the "high-value enterprise," requires skills of a different nature than those needed in the old high-volume mass production enterprises and is organized in a different way than the rigidly hierarchical structures that characterized standardized production.

To reiterate: the new information age enterprises not only require workers with different skills, organized differently from the industrial age companies, but the companies themselves obey new patterns of ownership and control, and hence of power. In the old high-volume enterprise the principal holders of power were those who owned the machines and those who ran them. However, in the new, information-age companies a steadily diminishing share of every dollar spent in an advanced economy has gone to production workers. Yet, those who conceptualize problems have commanded ever higher salaries and fees. In 1920, more than 85 percent of the cost of an automobile went to pay routine laborers and investors. By 1990, these two groups received less than 60 percent, with the remainder going to designers, engineers, stylists, planners, strategists, financial specialists, executive officers, lawyers, advertisers, marketers and the like. Today, not more than 3 percent of the price of a semiconductor chip goes to the owners of raw materials and energy, 5 percent to those who own the equipment and facilities, and 6 percent to routine labor. More than 85 percent is for specialized design and engineering services and for patents and copyrights on past discoveries made in the course of providing such services.[5]

There is an economic and power shift away from the old-line capitalists and their legions of unskilled and semi-skilled workers to a new class of managers and specialists whom Reich calls the "symbolic analysts" (more about this later). There is also a shift in the location of operations and controls in these new enterprises: the old line mass-production company may have had many foreign subsidiaries, but they were owned and controlled from corporate headquarters; furthermore, most products had distinct nationalities, and most of the work that went into these products was done in one place. However, all this is changing. In the emerging high-value economy, fewer products have distinct nationalities. Inputs can be produced efficiently in many different locations, to be combined in all sorts of ways to serve customer needs in many places. Intellectual and financial capital can come from anywhere, and be added instantly.[6]

Reich calls these new organizational setups "global webs" which have largely lost identity with, or allegiance to, any given nation-state. What is traded between nations is less often finished products than specialized problem solving (marketing, advertising, customer consulting) and brokerage (financing, searching, contracting) services, as well as certain routine components and services, all of which are combined to create value.[7]

In addition, one can begin to see a pattern emerging in the operations of these global webs. High-volume, standardized production occurs mainly in low-wage countries, with the exception of those goods that must be assembled in higher-wage nations where the final products are to be sold. Often it's cheaper to assemble the parts there because of protectionist barriers. High-value problem-solving, identifying and brokering occurs wherever useful insights can be found around the world.

The high-value global enterprise is evolving into an international partnership of skilled people whose insights are combined with one another and who contract with unskilled workers from around the world for whatever must be standardized and produced in high volume.[8]

These are some of the major characteristics of the emerging enterprises of the global information-age economy, and they differ in fundamental ways from their predecessors. Of course, the old mass production companies have not entirely disappeared; a number of them are still left in the U.S., although many have already moved to low-wage, Third-World countries or become largely automated, requiring few blue-collar workers.

It is not only the nature of manufacturing enterprises that is changing in the new global economy; whole sectors of the economy are undergoing fundamental shifts away from mass production industries located in the so-called developed countries, as well as other trends which will be discussed below. A good description of these shifts and the reasons for them is contained in another seminal work, Alvin Toffler's The Third Wave.[9]

In analyzing the status and changes in jobs, it is customary to use the economists' classification of work according to sectors of the economy. For many years, these sectors have been divided into three groups: the "primary" sector, agriculture and mining; the "secondary" sector, manufacturing; and the "services" sector, a catch-all category. The latter includes everything from health services, fast food restaurants, auto repair shops to highly skilled and remunerated professions: lawyers, doctors, university professors, engineers, etc. In 1850, the primary sector employed some 60 percent of the working population; now less than 3 percent are active in agriculture and mining. In 1960, some 25 percent of the work force was active in manufacturing. Now, some 16 percent of workers are employed in industries and the figure may shrink to 12 percent or less in the next 10 to 15 years, which would mean a further sharp downturn in the number of people employed in manufacturing work. The big area of employment has become the services sector, which now employs over 50 percent of the working population and accounts for approximately two-thirds of the U.S. gross domestic product.[10]

From the above figures, it should be fairly evident that these conventional ways of looking at the working population of this and other so-called industrialized countries has become increasingly inoperable, since the bulk of employment growth is occurring in the ill-defined catch-all category of "services". Service workers include janitors, domestic help, etc., as well as high-priced lawyers, stock brokers, college professors and a whole host of people who work in enterprises and institutions not engaged in agriculture, mining or manufacturing. Since some two-thirds of the American economy is now comprised of services, this category has become almost meaningless as a way to describe how people earn a living.

Some of the analysts who have dealt with this subject have dubbed the workers who are engaged in activities related to the new information-age economy "knowledge workers," or "Third Wave" employees; but in this writer's opinion, the most appropriate categorization of the work force of the future—not only in the U.S. but in other nations as well,—is in the three categories

Reich dubs <u>routine production services, in-person services</u> and <u>symbolic-analytic services</u>.

In Reich's classification of work, <u>routine production services</u> comprise all kinds of repetitive tasks performed in high-volume mass production. Workers in this category are the traditional blue-collar workers, often unionized, but also included are routine supervisory jobs performed by low and mid-level managers—foremen, line managers, clerical supervisors and section chiefs. These individuals perform repetitive checks on subordinates' work and enforce standard operating procedures. They also serve as information middle men, interpreting the directives sent down by top management and passing data collected by the troops upward to the decision-makers.

Another traditional category of work, <u>in-person services,</u> also entails fairly simple and repetitive tasks. According to Reich, the big difference between in-person services and routine production is that these services must be provided person-to-person and thus are not sold world-wide. Like routine production services, the pay of in-person services is a function of hours worked or amount of work performed, and many jobs in these categories do not demand advanced education; often a high school diploma or its equivalent and some vocational training are sufficient. Included in the in-person server category are retail sales workers, waiters and waitresses, hospital attendants and orderlies, janitors, cashiers, nursing-home aides, child-care workers, secretaries, security guards (a new and growing subcategory), flight attendants—the list goes on and on.

Finally, we come to the third category, which Reich calls <u>symbolic-analytic services</u>. These are the "winner" jobs in the information-age economy, and include problem-solving, problem-identifying and strategic-brokering jobs. This latter function is tied to the organization and operations of the information age enterprises (that will be discussed in more detail in Chapter 3). As Reich states:

> Like routine production services (but <u>unlike </u>in-person services), symbolic analytic services can be traded world-wide and thus must compete

with foreign providers even in the American
market. But they do not enter world commerce
as standardized things. Traded instead are the
manipulations of symbols—data, words, oral
and visual representations.[11]

Included in this category are "professional" jobs—scientists,
engineers, architects, doctors, lawyers and university professors.
It also includes activities in so-called "creative" fields, such as
writers and editors, journalists, media workers, advertising and
marketing executives and strategists as well as the upper ranks
of corporate America and their entourages. As Reich and other
writers point out, the future really belongs to those who can enter the ranks of symbolic analysts or their equivalent.

But what about the workers in the other two categories, particularly the so-called routine production workers who have often been portrayed as the "heroes" of the industrial age in both
capitalist and socialist societies? A number of books and articles published recently trace the declining prospects of routine
production workers who, in 1990, comprised about 25 percent of
the American work force. This decline has already occurred in
the case of workers in the agricultural sector. In the middle of
the last century some 60 percent of the entire U.S. work force
was employed in farming; now less than 2.7 percent are directly
employed in agriculture, and a great number of these workers
might properly be called symbolic analysts because they do not
toil in the fields but direct the operations of farms, dairies, food
storage and processing facilities and the like from air conditioned offices. Agriculture in the U.S. has become agri-
business: a small group of workers and managers account for
more than 20 percent of the gross national product; and with the
exciting prospects offered by biotechnology, this sector of the
economy will rapidly become even more high-tech.[12]

Much the same thing has happened to routine production
workers in the services sector. The armies of "back office"
clerks and mid-level paper shufflers, that used to be an essential
element in such fields as banking and insurance, have been re-

placed by computers, and more automation is on the drawing boards. In fact, such word and numerical processing jobs that used to offer many employment opportunities for high school graduates have either been largely automated out of existence in this country or sent overseas (with modern earth-to-satellite communications and jet airplanes it is possible to send data to Third World countries for overnight processing—often taking advantage of time differentials so that work sent out of the U.S. at the close of business can be processed overseas and be available in finished form the next morning in this country.)

The fate of routine production workers in the manufacturing sector is still not desperate, but the trends are not encouraging. In the 1950s, some 33 percent of the U.S. work force was employed in manufacturing; at the present, that figure has declined to 17 percent and many analysts, including this writer, believe that in the next 20 years employment in manufacturing might decline to about 5 percent, a figure comparable to the agricultural sector. At the same time, routine production jobs account for a small fraction of the cost of producing most items in the United States and other advanced nations. (According to Reich, this fraction will continue to decline sharply as computer-integrated robots take over.) In 1977, it took routine producers 35 hours to assemble an automobile in the United States; it is estimated that by the mid-1990s, Japanese-owned factories in America were producing finished automobiles using only eight hours of routine producer's time.[13] As the ranks of blue-collar workers are thinning, so also are the lower and middle-management positions involving routine production. Many of these jobs involved routine information processing and passing instructions up and down the hierarchical chain of command—work which can now be done by computers, or is eliminated due to the restructuring of the company along contemporary horizontal lines. The changes are extensively discussed by Peter Drucker in his recent books, such as <u>Managing in a Time of Great Change</u>.[14] The reduction in the ranks of routine production workers who generally have only a high-school education has been reflected in the paychecks of those who remain employed. Between 1973 and 1993, the real hourly wage of Americans without a high-school diploma fell from $11.85 an hour to $8.64 an hour. In the early 1970s, households in the top 5 percent of the income bracket earned 10 times more than those in the bottom 5 percent; today they make almost 15 times more. Similar trends are evident in Britain and even Sweden.

Workers have been further squeezed by the decline in manufacturing employment. Manufacturing employment in the United States fell by 1.4 million between 1978 and 1990. Frequently, those who lost their jobs were the unskilled, and when they found new work, it was usually at lower pay. The experience has now become familiar to middle managers, as evidenced by the recent major corporate layoffs. The failure of the industrial sector to generate new jobs has been a major cause of labor's economic problems, and according to Ethan Kapstein, some of America's social problems more generally. [15]

The decline in routine jobs has hurt men more than women and, in particular, Afro-American males from the inner cities, who left the countryside to find jobs in manufacturing plants during and after World War II. The plight of these workers and other inner-city ghetto residents has been extensively analyzed by William Julius Wilson, for example, who concludes that: many of today's problems in the inner-city ghetto neighborhoods. Crime, family dissolution, welfare, low levels of social organization, and so on are fundamentally the consequence of the disappearance of the routine production jobs many Afro-American males left the farm to take.[16] The advent of the high-tech global economy would appear to only aggravate these major social and economic upheavals.

If the fate of routine production workers were not bad enough, according to the "pessimistic" view, the future prospects are also dim for that other category of workers who, in the opinion of many analysts, belong to the losing side in the information age economy: the so-called in-person servers.

Reich points out that the boats of in-person servers are sinking as well, but somewhat more slowly and unevenly, than those of routine production workers. In 1990, in-person service workers performed about 30 percent of the jobs in America, and that percentage keeps growing. However, most in-person servers are paid at or just slightly above the minimum wage and many only work part-time; their take-home pay is modest, to say the least. Nor do they receive all the benefits (health care, life insurance, disability, and so forth) that routine producers in large manufacturing corporations or symbolic analysts receive. In-person servers are sheltered from the direct effects of global competition, but they are not immune to its indirect effects.[17]

Nor, I might add, are they immune from competition for the same jobs from recent immigrants—legal and often ille-gal—from Third World countries, who are prepared to work at extremely low wages. Furthermore, they must often compete with former routine production workers who have few alterna-tives but to seek in-person service jobs, as well as the wives of such refugees from routine production who enter the job market to help their spouses keep the family income up to previous lev-els.

As I have already noted, in 1990 some 55 percent of all U.S. jobs were performed by routine production workers and in-person servers, and their prospects are not bright. What percent-age of the U.S. population do the families of such workers repre-sent? The answer is hard to come by, especially if one looks to the future. However, a number of experts believe that only about 20 percent of America's children are being prepared for the "good" symbolic analyst jobs and that, at the maximum, only 20 percent to 30 percent of the adult population in the U.S. will be engaged in such work. I will discuss in some detail in Chap-ter 3 the symbolic analysts or knowledge workers, whose future prospects are indeed bright.

This chapter is devoted to the darker view of the future and to those workers who are on the wrong side of change. The ex-perts who belong to the pessimistic camp have come up with a number of scenarios, almost all of them dismal: not just about the fate of these workers, but of the American economy as well. If these workers cease to hold well-paying jobs or become per-manently unemployed, the consumer base and, consequently, the whole economy of the country could be dealt a serious blow. In addition, a number of writers, including Robert Reich, talk of the "secession" of the symbolic analysts. What is meant here is not only that such favored families move into homogenous enclaves ("lifestyle enclaves" to use Christopher Lasch's term) which are frequently located in the suburbs or exurbs, but that the symbolic analysts also disengage from the broader public in many other ways, including withdrawal from public schools and other community organizations. Symbolic analysts often lose ties to their own nations, becoming global nomads, loyal only to their profession or career and their luxurious cosmopolitan lifestyles which they share with the "yuppies" of other nations. These developments may lead to a situation with which this author is quite familiar, having spent many years working to promote the economic and social development of Latin America. There one can often find rigidly two-tiered societies consisting of the rich who are educated abroad and enjoy contemporary lifestyles, living in luxury behind high walls, surrounded by a great mass of people living in poverty and ignorance. Despite all development efforts, this duality of the "haves" and "have-nots" persists and often grows.

To avoid such a tragic fate for the U.S., a number of recently published books and articles offer suggestions for measures to be taken to ward off the inevitable decline in the fortunes of most Americans. As Ethan Kapstein stated in a recent article:

> The world may be moving inexorably toward one of those tragic moments that will lead future historians to ask, why was nothing done in time? Were the economic and policy elites unaware of the profound disruption that economic and technological changes were causing men and women? What prevented them from taking steps necessary to prevent a global social crisis?
>
> … The global economy is leaving millions of disaffected workers in its train. Inequality, unemployment, and endemic poverty have become

its hand maidens. Rapid technological change and heightening international competition are fraying job markets of the major industrialized countries. At the same time, systemic pressures are curtailing every government's ability to respond with new spending. Just when working people most need the nation-state as a buffer from the world economy, it is abandoning them.[18]

Notwithstanding Kapstein's prediction that "national responses to this global problem are likely to fail, as any state that deviates from 'responsible' economic policies will be punished by currency markets and bondholders," other experts have offered suggestions for remedial action for a situation they regard as exceedingly grave. Robert Reich, Jeremy Rifkin and William Julius Wilson I have already mentioned, but others include such highly credentialed analysts as Thomas Donahue, former President of the AFL-CIO, Robert Lawrence, and Summer Rosen.[19] In order to give the reader some idea of the nature of such policy recommendations, I have taken a representative sample from a dozen experts, from fairly middle-of-the-road prescriptions for increased education and training to bring the American work force up to the standards demanded by a global information age economy to far-out solutions involving the provision of life-long guaranteed incomes and make-work job programs reminiscent of the Depression-era WPA projects.

Grouped according to subject matter and tabulated according to the number of times each recommendation or a similar one is mentioned, the results are as follows:

(a) <u>Increased welfare programs (13 mentions)</u>
Relocation grants, publicly financed low-cost rental housing, free child-care services, universal health care, expanded earned-income tax credit program, subsidized transportation of inner city workers to the suburbs, etc.

(b) Education, training and research (9 mentions)
Subsidies for education, training and retraining programs, funding for basic research for such programs, establishing national performance standards for secondary schools and providing government financial assistance to meet such standards.

(c) Infrastructure and other public works programs (6 mentions)
Improving the nation's physical infrastructure (roads, bridges, etc.) and WPA-style public work programs (labor-intensive, minimum-wage public service jobs of last resort).

(d) Subsidies to industries and other stimulants (5 mentions)
Public subsidies to firms for "high-value" production, programs to ease the transition out of "sunset" industries, tax incentives for research and development, employee training, etc. and fiscal and monetary policies to stimulate job creation.

(e) Job-sharing, shorter work-week, etc. (4 mentions)
This category is self-explanatory and includes policies to spread the available work around to the maximum number of workers.

(f) International political and economic measures (5 mentions)
International coordination of labor demands, policy coordination to develop expansionary policies within a collective framework, changing U.S. trade policies toward managed trade, as well as managing currency and investment flows to protect U.S. workers.

(g) Domestic political action (4 mentions)

Several experts call for a revival of populist movements to restrict immigration, foster "positive economic nationalism," etc.

(h) Dis-incentives for business (4 mentions)
Tax dis-incentives for replacement of people by machines and use of low-cost overseas labor, "social controls," such as re-regulation of businesses and "evaluation" of job-destroying technologies, mergers and acquisitions.

(i) Guaranteed income schemes (3 mentions)
Programs to establish national guaranteed incomes to meet all basic nutritional, housing, health and recreational requirements, programs to issue scrip to be exchanged for fundamental maintenance (food, clothing, shelter), etc.

(j) Subsidies to the "Third Sector" or NGO'S (2 mentions)
Several experts suggest that the so-called Third Sector or non-profit organizations could be strengthened through public subsidies for job creation as an alternative to welfare grants.

(k) Other recommendations
In this category fall such suggestions as profit-sharing plans for workers to participate in productivity gains, programs of universal public service and promotion of community life.

These recommendations vary greatly and cover a wide range of social and economic policies, but they all share one characteristic: their implementation on a national scale will likely prove to be extremely expensive. Unfortunately, few of the writers I have cited in this chapter include in their analyses an estimation of the financial costs of their recommendations, but some experts include statements to the effect that significant government funds would be required for their implementation.

Two experts who attempt to quantify in a rough fashion the costs of some of their policy suggestions are Ethan Kapstein and

William Julius Wilson. Kapstein, in a far-ranging article on workers and the world economy, estimates that the cost for retraining workers in the U.S., with its 7 million unemployed, would be $49 billion. "Today, the U.S. government spends about $10 billion on work-related education and training. In the current fiscal environment, it is difficult to imagine that number rising by the required amount."[20]

Wilson, another highly regarded analyst of joblessness in this country, especially in the inner cities, considers that "[t]he cost of retraining is considerable and none of the industrial democracies has advanced convincing proposals indicating how to implement such a program effectively." In connection with one of his "immediate solutions" to the jobs problem in the United States, a suggested WPA-style program of employment of last resort, he admits that such a program "will not be cheap .... Including the costs of supervisors and materials, it is estimated that each subminimum-wage WPA-style job would cost at least $12,000. That would represent $12 billion for every 1 million jobs created."[21]

Even a fairly non-controversial policy recommendation, such as retraining for unemployed workers, carries a worrisome price tag, and the full range of suggestions put forth by the experts cited might reach unprecedentedly high figures. In the present climate of fiscal restraint, such programs would be politically unfeasible; but even should domestic economic and political pressures build up to the point that the government authorities would have to initiate such programs or risk social and economic chaos (as some ultra-left writers predict), a question remains as to whether such ambitious programs could be financed, short of raising taxes to a confiscatory level or through reckless deficit financing such as has taken place in Latin America in the post- World War II era. This question may appear entirely hypothetical, since reliable cost estimates of such job programs are lacking; but, in reality, it goes to the heart of any consideration of policy recommendations in this sensitive area. Furthermore, there is a new factor to be considered in this respect: the growing role of the global financial market in determining economic policy measures of nation-states (I shall discuss this in Chapter 4).

At the same time, a legitimate question arises as to whether the situation of systemic future unemployment is as grave as has been presented by the "pessimistic" writers cited above. The next chapter will present the views of a number of distinguished writers who claim that the situation is quite different from that described by the pessimistic camp, apparently rendering the above-mentioned policy recommendations unnecessary and perhaps even harmful to the economy. Faced with this dilemma of clashing views, let me urge the reader to remember a point I made earlier about the tendency of many experts to focus only on a few aspects of a complex problem, those which are congenial to them and fit in with their overall world view. Such is the case with the "pessimists" and "optimists" discussed in this book. Both camps present compelling arguments for their conclusions and recommendations which may constitute equally valid, although limited, explanations of what is going on in this country during a time of revolutionary change. Apropos of this, I am reminded of the opening lines of Charles Dickens's novel A Tale of Two Cities, which describes life in France and England during the time of the French Revolution:

> It was the best of times, it was the worst of times.... We had everything before us, we had nothing before us, we were all going direct to Heaven, we were all going direct the other way.

I believe that we are experiencing another such time of great anxieties and great expectations—the loss of one set of approaches and solutions to life and the advent of new ones. I will develop this theme in later chapters, but first let us turn to that group of pundits who see nothing but a rosy future ahead.

Chapter 3

The Optimists' Vision

The last chapter outlined the thoughts of leading writers who view the future of the U.S. economy and that of most American workers with dismay and foreboding. We now turn to the optimists' camp—those who see a promising future ahead for the economy and for workers as well. Some of these writers border on the euphoric in their descriptions of life in the 21st century, including Dr. Michael G. Zey, who begins his recent work with the following thundering statement.

> The human species is about to burst the boundaries of nature and unleash the power of its technology and human ingenuity, hurtling itself into the next stage of its evolution. In doing so, it will fulfill its destiny to expand its own capabilities and enhance the planet and the universe. Humanity is programmed, genetically perhaps, for growth and progress. Unlike other species, humanity cannot and will not stand still. [1]

Most people might prefer a more restrained presentation of the optimist's view of the future, yet it is hard to find understatements in a field of superlatives. For example, the lead article in the July 1997 issue of <u>Wired</u> by Peter Schartz and Peter Leyden:

> A bad meme—a contagious idea—began spreading through the United States in the 1980's: America is in decline, the world is going to hell, and our children's lives will be worse than our own. The particulars are now familiar: good jobs are disappearing, working people are falling into poverty, the underclass is swelling, crime is out of control. The post-Cold War world is fragmenting, and conflicts are

erupting all over the planet. The environment is imploding—with global warming and ozone depletion we'll all either die of cancer or live in <u>Waterworld</u>. As for our kids, the collapsing educational system is producing either gun-toting gangsters or burger-flipping dopes who can't read.

The authors point out that by the late 1990s, another world view began to gain ground, born of the surging stock market and a booming economy. America is finally getting its economic act together, the world is not such a dangerous place after all, and the kids just might lead tolerable lives. Yet the good times will come only to a privileged few—a fortunate fifth of our society—the vast majority in the United States and the world face a dire future of increasingly desperate poverty. And the environment? In their view, it's a lost cause.

But in the optimist's view, we are watching the beginnings of a global economic boom on a scale never experienced before, a period of sustained growth that could eventually double the world's economy every dozen years and bring increasing prosperity for—quite literally—billions of people on the planet. We are riding the early waves of a 25-year run of a greatly expanding economy that will do much to solve problems like poverty and ease tensions throughout the world. In the developed countries new technology will continue to develop through the early part of the 21st century. And then the process of globalization, the opening up of national economies and the integration of markets, will drive the growth through much of the rest of the world. In their view, an unprecedented alignment of an ascendant Asia, a revitalized America, and a reintegrated greater Europe— including a recovered Russia—together will create an economic juggernaut that pulls along most other regions of the planet. "These two metatrends—fundamental technological change and a new ethos of openness—will transform our world into the beginnings of a global civilization, a new civilization of civilizations, that will blossom through the coming century".[2]

The authors develop a rosy scenario (a term much used by futurists) of a truly better world by the year 2020, the fundamental concepts of which can be summarized as follows:

During the period 1980-2020, a remarkable transformation will take place in the world's economies, driven by the waves of new technology which will be developed and implemented during the early parts of the 21st century. The basic science is now in place for five successive waves of technology—computers, telecommunications, biotechnology, nanotechnology and alternative energy—which will lead to big productivity increases, and these, in turn, will produce high rates of economic growth. (I will discuss the idea of breakthrough technologies and economic growth in more detail in Chapter 6.) This growth should quickly spread from the highly developed countries throughout the world due to another process currently underway: the relentless process of globalization—the opening up of national economies and the integration of markets. "An unprecedented alignment of an ascendant Asia, a revitalized America, and a reintegrated greater Europe—including a recovered Russia—together will create an economic juggernaut that pulls along most other regions of the planet."[3]

The scenario predicts 25 years of prosperity combined with a benign affect on the environment, leading to unprecedented rates of economic growth. From an average increase of the world's gross domestic product of 3 percent during most of the 1970s, all the 1980s and the early 1990s, the rate would rise by 2005 to an astounding 6 percent. If this growth rate continues, the size of the global economy would double in 12 years, and double twice in just 25 years. Such a cornucopia of wealth would provide ample resources to solve some of society's seemingly intractable social problems and embark on new initiatives such as those outlined in Chapter 2 of this book, not just in the United States but globally.

This is the gist of the argument for a highly optimistic view of economic developments presented in this article and similar recent publications. Other equally buoyant predictions come from the futurists Alvin and Heidi Toffler, authors of Future Shock and The Third Wave. Their recent publication, Creating a New Civilization, begins with the following astounding statement:

> A new civilization is emerging in our lives, and blind men everywhere are trying to suppress it. This new civilization brings with it new family styles, changed ways of working, loving and living, a new economy, new political conflicts and beyond all this an altered consciousness... the Second Wave—the rise of industrial civilization—took a mere three hundred years. Today history is more accelerative, and it is likely that the Third Wave will sweep across history and complete itself in a few decades... The Third Wave brings with it a genuinely new way of life based on diversified, renewable energy

sources; on methods of production that make most factory assembly lines obsolete; on new, non-nuclear families; on a novel institution that might be called the "electronic college" and on radically changed schools and corporations of the future.[4]

Another strong statement of what is underway in the world's economy and its effect on us all comes from Walter B. Wriston, former chairman of Citicorp and one of the most innovative financiers of our time, in the preface to his book, The Twilight of Sovereignty:

Historians looking back on events from the perspective of many years often give names to eras that contemporaries living through those times never contemplated. Several hundred years passed before the eras we now know as the Middle Ages, the Renaissance, and the Reformation got their names. Today the case can be made that we do not have to wait for some future historian to name the age in which we are living: It is the Information Age. The evidence is plain to see everywhere around us. The world is now tied together by an electronic network that carries news and data, good and bad, true or false, with the speed of light anywhere on this planet. The massive amounts of information that move over the network, combined with the speed of transmission, are transforming the way the world works in ways at least as profound as occurred in the Industrial Revolution.... The perception of what constitutes an asset, and what it is that creates wealth is shifting dramatically. Intellectual capital is becoming relatively more important than physical capital. Indeed, the new source of wealth is not material, it is information, knowledge applied to work to create value. [5]

Since this new source of wealth is based on a non-material and ever-expanding resource, in Wriston's view it can create a cornucopia of opportunities for the production of wealth and prosperity unprecedented in human history.

Another slightly less euphoric statement of the prospects for a prosperous future, at least for some nations and individuals, is in the introductory chapter of Michael Moynihan's The Coming American Renaissance:

> The America that actually exists, the one de-scribed by objective statistics and that you can see when you walk out the door, is not in decline or on the verge of catastrophe. By any objective measure, the U.S. economy is thriving. Economic performance in recent years has not just been good, it has been better than in any comparable period of the postwar era.... But the current cyclical recovery is only a part of a larger story, the one I intend to tell in this book. For behind the current recovery lies a far greater phenomenon, that of America's long-term economic resurgence. From out of the turmoil of the 1980s and the crucible of the last recession, America has reinvented its economy. While the recovery has gotten little respect at home, it has taken the world by storm. Called Rising Sam in Japan, America is commanding new respect. What has changed about the U.S. economy in the last few years? New technologies, the end of the Cold War, and demographic changes, combined with uncommon natural advantages have put the United States back in the driver's seat. The story of this resurgence is one of economic opportunity for individual Americans. [6]

However, he warns that: The future will not reward those who resist change. Rather it will reward those who adapt most rapidly, whether they are countries, companies or people. The years ahead will not be calm or devoid of crisis. The Italian Renaissance was a period of excitement and turmoil, too. It was a time that witnessed great art and architecture, important scientific discoveries, the first trips to America and Asia and an explosion of trade, but it was also a time of war, political upheaval, social dislocation, and occasional calamities. It was not Utopian. Nevertheless, it was a period of rapid advancement for humanity. By comparison, the pace of political change over the next quarter century will be slow, but intellectual, scientific and organizational change will occur rapidly. [7]

These are fair samples of the visionary and highly positive views prevalent in the camp of the optimists. At the same time, there is another group of writers who content themselves with refuting, through statistical analyses, pessimistic visions such as those mentioned in Chapter 2. The right-wing think tank, the American Enterprise Institute, has brought out a recent series of studies on understanding economic inequality which deals with trends in the level and distribution of U.S. wages, income, wealth, consumption and other measures of material welfare, as well as highlighting important questions future interpretations, causation and consequences.[8] Of particular note is a study by Richard Burkhauser which deals with the widespread impression in the United States that the middle class is gradually disappearing, as declining real incomes force more and more families into the lower-income category while others—a much smaller number—rise into the class of the "rich". Without going into details of the methodology used in this study, it is interesting that the author selects starting and ending dates of his assessment of movements between income classes and the changing distribution of income in the 1980s in careful correlation to the business cycle peaks and troughs in this period (1979 to 1989). His data shows, first, that from the business cycle peak of 1979 to the peak in 1989, real income rose for the top 70 percent of the income distribution, not just the very rich as has been widely asserted. Comparing business cycle trough to trough, incomes rose for 90 percent of the families. Second, the proportion of families with middle class incomes did indeed decline somewhat in the 1980s—from 50.5 percent in 1979 to 47.1 percent by 1989. However, contrary to the conventional wisdom, this decline was not because millions of families lost income and slipped down to the "lower" income class. Instead, comparing 1979 with 1989, 92 percent of those who moved out of the middle class <u>moved up, not down.</u>[9]

Other writers in the AEI series deals such diverse topics as relative wage trends—especially those of women—developments in productivity and wage inequality, aspects of public attitudes toward inequality of income and wealth, wage inequality in various countries, inequality based on consumption and inequality of income vs. distribution of wealth.

Without prejudice to the merits of this series of publications, designed to improve public discussion of issues of economic inequality which, as the studies' foreword states, "are often partial and partisan and often superficial," I must admit to a certain skepticism about their results (as well as the statistical analyses produced by the pessimists cited in Chapter 2). Having dealt with statistics of various sorts during my 30-year career in international banking, I have a great respect for the uses and abuses of these data, which are often employed to buttress preconceived positions on a matter under discussion and, therefore I will abstain from involvement in the "war of numbers" which has developed over the question of the future of work. Moreover, the purpose of this book is to discuss not statistics but competing visions of the future, an activity that is essentially subjective in nature although ideally based on "unusual discernment or foresight"—to quote Webster's dictionary.

To return to the discussion of the optimist's camp, their position might be summarized as follows. The new advances in science and technology and the liberating effects of the growing global economy now and in the future will, to an increasing extent, create new job opportunities and enormous gains in productivity which, in turn, will translate into the creation of wealth on an unprecedented scale and thus allow for a substantial improvement in the living standards and welfare of most Americans. These advances will be largely achieved without government intervention and, hence, the proper role of government will be to foster this process by making such investments in public goods and services as to bolster these revolutionary advances in growth and development, as well as supporting market forces through further deregulation and tax abatements. A corollary of this view is that those forces which create great opportunities for progress are also destructive of the existing order ("creative destruction" to use economist Joseph Schumpeter's term). They sweep away old ways of doing things, old relationships and roles, not just for governments and organizations, but also for families and individuals. To resist these forces, as the Luddites did in the 18th century, is futile and self-destructive; the only way to survive and prosper in this situation is to adapt to the new economy.

But what about those people who do not have the financial, physical or mental capacities to adapt to this fast-paced, highly competitive, entrepreneurial society? In general, the optimists have little to say on this subject, just as the pessimists tend to ignore or underplay the evident economic costs of the remedies they have prescribed for just such persons who will have difficulty adapting to the requirements of the post-industrial age.

Some in the optimist camp have attempted to address the plight of the "losers" in this new high-tech world; Walter B. Wriston has this to say:

> Not everyone is fully plugged in to the global conversation [the new information age economy] or equipped to take full advantage of it. Those who fully participate in the information economy benefit most from it... These people, on the whole, will be internationalists in their outlook and will approve or encourage the worldwide erosion of traditional sovereignty. They will feel more affinity to their fellow global conversationalists than those of their

countrymen who are not part of the global conversation. These latter will have little stake in the global conversation and may come to hate it and those who participate in it as they realize that in all this talk they are rarely mentioned and then only as a social problem. All technological progress has created social problems, and the information revolution moving over the global network is no exception. New skills and new insights will be required to survive and prosper and those who do not or cannot adapt will be left behind with all the social trauma that entails. [10]

Others, while acknowledging that change causes social traumas, urge a positive attitude toward events which they regard as inevitable. One such writer is Newt Gingrich:

Our grandchildren will be comfortable in a world where every business, community and citizen must adapt or pay the price of obsolescence. They will value successful change and successful adaptation because there is a deep need in the younger generation to affirm their intuition that there must be more to life than standing in line at the steelworkers' union hall for unemployment checks or getting drunk at a local bar discussing the unlikely chance that their steel mill may reopen.

Rather than whining that change is frightening (which it is), that change often disassociates us from our roots (which it does), and that change sometimes has undesirable side effects (which is true), our grandchildren will accept these caveats as facts of life. They will ask their culture to teach them how to rise above these difficulties rather than hide from them. [11]

37

In all fairness to Gingrich, he goes on to suggest a series of measures involving mainly adult re-training and re-education, to ease the transition to the new "opportunity society." But he comes back, again and again, to his bright vision of the future:

> A cultural bias toward a more pessimistic, more defensive view of the future runs very deep in the American Left. As a result, the Left has been consistently wrong in recent years about the likelihood of jobs being created by technology.
>
> Every major technological breakthrough, from internal-combustion engines to computers, has ultimately created jobs. Furthermore, the new jobs have ultimately been better and more humanizing than those of the previous culture.... For two hundred years, people throughout the Western world have moved toward higher technology and better paying, cleaner, more humane jobs. [12]

In this same vein and in even more forceful language, Professor Richard B. McKenzie lays out the law for both blue- collar and white-collar workers. He argues that a new economic frontier is opening up as the rapid growth of electronic technology creates fresh room for growth and creativity. However, this progress does not come without a social cost, the rapidity with which capital has become more mobile and forced a restructuring of business around the world has, no doubt, undermined the employment security of workers. In his view, it has forced many American workers to give up prized jobs with what were perceived to be invulnerable firms that, because of their market position, could "over pay" in cash and benefits. It has also forced American workers to compete with other, often lower-paid, workers from around the world for the jobs and wages they covet.

He poses the question: "What should workers do to counter the economic tectonics afoot in the world?" We can all lament the affected workers' hardship, but there is little that affected workers or anyone else can do about the matter—other than not waste a lot of energy fighting the forces afoot. His message is that we must adjust—will adjust, as we always have—in spite of the grumbling that always tends to accompany adjustments to externally imposed demands. In MacKenzie's view, there isn't really much that governments can do to hold the forces at bay (other than get out of the way) or to bring back workers' lost security, because governments also have, in the process, become competitors for capital resources and face many of the same types of constraints that workers do: "The writing is on the (international) walls for all workers of the world to follow: *Become more productive. Work harder and smarter. Get more education and skills. Get competitive. Do more than others have been doing or will likely do. Stop complaining.*"[13]

And so in the writings of the optimists' camp we have gone from Karl Marx's admonition to the workers of the world to unite and throw off the shackles of capitalism to McKenzie's advice: adapt and stop complaining—there's no escaping global capitalism.

This writer agrees with McKenzie that the wave of the future involves a high-tech global economy which will successfully exploit the tremendous advances in scientific and technological knowledge to produce unprecedented levels of wealth. However, I do not share McKenzie's optimism in believing that the grave social problems caused by the changes inherent in such fundamental shifts can be easily overcome by market forces alone. In this respect, the pessimists are right in their concern for the social dimensions of these revolutionary changes in the way we live and work.

Finally, no discussion of the economic future would be complete without a mention of another recent revolutionary development: the growing role of international capital markets in determining the economic policies of supposedly sovereign nation-states. This development has a direct bearing on the discussion of the future of work, as will be shown in the next chapter.

Chapter 4

A New Policy Player: The Global Capital Market

Powered by a technological revolution that has resulted in the cost of communicating and computing effectively going to near zero, the capital markets are approaching at breakneck speed the single market conditions long ago predicted by economist Adam Smith. The enormous analytic power and richness of information available to capital market participants have finally made the theoretical techniques of isolating risk a reality. Technology has also enabled the transfer of capital market know-how to virtually every corner of the world. The result is a market that knows no master: a market that will integrate developed and developing countries alike, deploy the national savings of nations rich with baby boomers to new distant venues, and will defy the control of every government in the world.

Ted Hall from the Introduction
to "Market Unbound"

The previous chapters have dealt with the effects, both positive and negative, of the information revolution on employment, primarily in the U.S. In this chapter, we shall discuss fundamental and far-reaching changes in the money markets of the world and the ability of sovereign states to control their own economies. As former Secretary of the Treasury W. Michael Blumenthal has stated, in the financial marketplace, technology—the ability to develop and gain access to vast data bases, to handle complex computing with lightning speed, and to communicate instantaneously—has had a profound impact on the economy in at least four critically important ways. First, information is now universally available, in real time, simultaneously, in every financial center of the world. Second, technology has tied all principal countries and world financial and banking centers together into one integrated network. Few countries or parts of the world can remain insulated from financial shocks and changes, wherever they may occur. Third, technology has made possible the establishment of a new, comprehensive system and highly efficient world market to match lenders and borrowers, to pool resources and share risk on an international scale, without regard to national boundaries. Finally, technology has engendered a vast amount of innovation or new "products," mostly to hedge against changes in interest rates or exchange rates.

In his view, technology has made the system more efficient, but new systemic and policy problems have also been raised, as the recent unstable performance of the securities markets clearly showed. The problem lies in the public sector and in our political and institutional framework, where adaptation to technological change is slow and where obsolete institutions and outmoded rules create the uncertainty and tensions that have adversely affected the quality of macroeconomic management in our newly pluralistic world. [1]

Blumenthal develops the concept of the waning of the nation-state: "The logic of the electronics revolution leads to a first conclusion which is basic to everything else... that technology is rapidly making the basic notion of national sovereignty obsolete in many areas of economic affairs." He poses these questions:

If there is now one world capital market, how then can any major nation hope to conduct a truly effective national monetary policy all on its own?

If exchange rates quickly transmit the effects of key tax, spending and budget decisions from one major country to another, how then can there be a truly independent national fiscal policy? If factors of production are less fixed and knowledge flows freely across borders, how then can strictly national rules

42

and regulations remain effective if they are out of step with the rest of the world?

And, if technology can rapidly override the effects, how can national import restrictions and protectionism possibly still achieve their stated aims?

In conclusion, technology has created a world no longer effectively composed of individual national economic entities. Thus, if we in the U.S. continue to act as if nothing has changed, our persistence in applying strictly national policies is bound to prove frustrating, and often counterproductive.

We will discuss these concepts later in this chapter, but first, it might help our understanding of these truly revolutionary developments in the political economy of nations if we briefly trace the historical development of the modern international capital market from its origins in the early post World War II era.

Many observers believe that the global money market as we know it today had its beginnings in the early 1950's, ironically enough in an attempt of the revolutionary Chinese to evade the measures taken by the U.S. government to freeze Chinese accounts in American banks. The Chinese transferred their dollar accounts to a Russian-owned bank in France, not a fool-proof measure since these accounts could still be seized by the French government. In turn, the Soviet government decided to transfer its dollar holdings to an even safer haven, to a subsidiary of their own bank in the City of London, the Moscow Narodny Bank. At that time, the City of London was a self-governing financial enclave that provided both banking secrecy and protection from any outside incursions that would threaten the viability of bank accounts. This new system was dubbed the Eurodollar market, the great technological breakthrough of international finance in the mid-twentieth century.

The so-called Eurodollar market is a market in international debt. It accepts deposits and makes loans which may, in principle, be designated in any currency of any country, provided only that the named currency is sufficiently "safe" to be internationally acceptable. The named currency would also have to be convertible to other main currencies, at exchange rates not subject to too violent or too unpredictable changes. In practice, the most likely currencies to be designated are U.S. dollars, British sterling, German marks, Swiss francs, or Japanese yen, with dollars still favored.

The market now extends far beyond its original location in Europe, with centers open for business almost any time elsewhere in the world. The terms "zeno-financing" and "zeno-markets," proposed by Fritz Machlup as an alternative to "Euro," have the merit of emphasizing the common feature of participating institutions, namely the use of currencies other than that of the country of domicile.

Taken as a whole, it is possible to distinguish four separate elements in Eurodollar finance. First, there is an inter-bank market, in which the participating financial institutions make deposits and borrow among themselves; the typical transaction appears to be short term. The second element covers the acceptance of deposits from, and the granting of loans to, financial institutions not participating in the market and to governments and companies. These transactions involve loans for longer periods than is usually the case in the interbank market. The third element is the so-called Eurobond market, in which placements provide an alternative means for the financing of government and company spending to that offered by direct lending from the participating banks. Finally, there is the foreign exchange market in which participating institutions, borrowers and lenders establish the relativities for the currencies in which transactions are undertaken. In a most important sense, a foreign exchange element is embodied each time a deposit, loan or bond placement is negotiated.

Characteristics of the Eurodollar Market:

1.An inter-bank market with typically large transactions. In other words, a wholesale market for a small number of operators: commercial banks, central banks, other financial non-bank institutions, large firms (especially transnational companies), and some very wealthy individuals. All, or almost all, transactions are inter-bank; non-bank operators normally deal through banks.

2. A largely unregulated market. The participating banks are not limited by reserve requirements, which set a ceiling on loans and are expensive. Taxes, if any, are light, business is covered by banking confidentiality and, therefore, the statistical coverage is poor. If bank examiners in an offshore center question the soundness of loans, the adequacy of the capital base, or the ethics of some transactions, it is possible to shift some or all of the business to another offshore center where bank examiners are less inquisitive.

3. An international offshore money market exists wherever dealing occurs throughout the world, and on a 24-hour basis. Essentially that is wherever telecommunications exist, for trading today is no longer limited to dealing rooms or the facilities of companies. While in the early days the market was essentially in London, today trading also centers in New York, a number of major European cities, Tokyo, Hong Kong and Singapore, with a network of smaller, secondary exchanges in virtually every country, including China and the former Soviet Union.

These markets are all interlinked, with business flowing from one into another and vice-versa. As one market closes, another opens up, starting with the closing quotations of the earlier market. For the sake of simplicity, the trading may be viewed as starting in Japan, where "the sun rises."

The Japanese market, of which Tokyo is preeminent, is high-volume, related mainly to the needs of banks' commercial customers. This involves principally U.S. dollar/yen trading because of the very large amount of commerce between the two countries. Unlike some markets, Tokyo closes at a set time in the afternoon, a custom that has hampered its growth.

The Singapore and Hong Kong markets open one hour after Tokyo. These centers are less regulated and more freewheeling, as both localities, desirous of becoming international financial centers as one base for their economies, have sought to establish friendly banking and commercial environments. They have been very successful in their endeavors; many banks have opened foreign branches in both centers, which now have active foreign exchange markets where many currencies are traded.

Next on the circuit is Europe, the largest market, with principal centers in Great Britain, the Federal Republic of Germany and Switzerland. European banks have no set closing time and can trade 24 hours if they choose. The New York market opens next, although some dealers have been operating 24 hours in order to be in on the action in other markets firsthand and to avoid overnight positions. The West Coast markets are essentially tied into the New York center.

The technology and equipment used in the major trading offices are generally state-of-the-art, with the latest in computers and telecommunications and satellite links, so that messages can be sent instantaneously around the globe. Sophisticated encryption equipment is widely used, since financial transactions are often encoded to guard secrecy. All records are kept on computer tapes or discs capable of rapid erasure to guard against unauthorized personnel (particularly government inspectors) getting their hands on them. Also, duplicate records are often kept simultaneously in at least two places in the world, one location of which is secret, again to guard against unauthorized seizure.

Growth of the Market

As mentioned above, this worldwide money market had its origins in the mid-1950's as a result of the exigencies of the Cold War. Whatever the initial need that called forth the market, it grew slowly in the 1950s, then picked up speed as the U.S. balance-of-payments deficits increased in the 1960s, and holders of dollars chose to deposit them in banks outside the United States. From 1965 to 1971, the market grew at a compound annual rate of 37 percent. The market grew even more in the 1970s, fueled by the Arab nations' deposits of petrodollars in European banks for political reasons (i.e. to avoid embargoes by the U.S. government).

An idea of the rapid growth of the Euro-currency market can be gained from the following chart. Bear in mind that statistics on this market are hard to come by and can be misleading due to the problem of double counting of deposits in the system. However, a reliable source has developed the following table which shows Eurocurrency assets or liabilities of banks in European centers at end of period, net of double counting.

Year	Size ($US Billion)
1964	11.6
1965	14.5
1966	17.4
1967	20.8
1968	29.7
1969	44.0
1970	57.0
1971	71.0
1972	92.0
1973	132.0
1974	177.0
1975	205.0
1976	247.0
1977	300.0

1978*	377.0
1979	475.0

*First Quarter

Some idea of the importance of the Euro-currency market in the world economy can be had by comparing Euro-currencies and world currency reserves. According to one estimate, in 1977 the Euro-currency market's net size world-wide slightly exceeded $400 billion; whereas world currency reserves in central banks in that year reached only $300 billion. In the 1980s and 1990s the size and diversity of what now should properly be called the modern international capital market continued to grow by leaps and bounds, far outdistancing any efforts of central bankers to influence the market, much less any attempt to regulate it.

> As Walter B. Wriston described it:
> From [a] small beginning has grown a market that is truly something new under the sun. It is now a vital part of the international financial structure of the world, vastly increased in size and speed by the increasing facility of electronic markets and the increasingly global character of the world commerce.
>
> The Euro-currency markets are part of a global financial network that moves capital where it is needed and appreciates faster and more efficiently than ever before. But their very existence is a symbol of the growing futility of government attempts to regulate capital. These markets grew ... out of a failed attempt to control capital in ways it can no longer be controlled. [2]

Wriston holds that the Euro-currency market is a part of an even larger global financial network. The current size of this network can be gained from a 1996 <u>New York Times</u> estimate that "each day $3.2 <u>trillion</u> cascades through the world's foreign exchange settlement systems." Compare this to the fact that for the year 1995, the total gross domestic product (GDP) of the U.S.—the sum of all goods and services produced in the country during the entire year—was $7.3 trillion.[3] The huge size of the international money market far exceeds the need to finance trade between countries. According to Walter Wriston, capital transactions are now probably forty or fifty times greater than trade flows and have taken on a life of their own. One of the off-shoots of these markets is that the very efficiency of the system undermines or complicates national monetary and fiscal policies in particular countries. According to Wriston, in the international financial markets today, a vote on the soundness of each country's fiscal and monetary policies, in comparison with those of every other country in the world, is held in the trading rooms of the world every minute of every day. Every kind of information moves across the electronic infrastructure that binds the world together. The latest political joke makes its way from trading room to trading room around the world in minutes. The newest figures on the GNP (gross national product), the money supply, or the words of a political leader all enter the data bases that move markets. This continuing direct plebiscite on the value of currencies and commodities proceeds by methods that are growing more sophisticated every day.

In his view, even though Americans have accepted the ballot box as the arbiter of who holds office, this new global vote on the nation's fiscal and monetary policies is profoundly disturbing to many. Accepting the judgment of thousands of traders who translate the politicians' actions into new values for currencies is harder to accept because it developed so fast and is new and unfamiliar. Nevertheless, it is about as useful to curse the thermometer for recording a heat wave as it is to rail against the values the global market puts on a nation's currency. There is no escaping the system. [4]

In a New York Times article, Thomas L. Friedman referred to a failed attempt on the part of the world's largest central banks, led by the Federal Reserve, to try to prop up the dollar which was under attack by speculators in July 1994.[5] At that time, global currency markets were trading about $1 trillion each day, and these central banks "dug deep into their pockets and came up with about $5 billion and change which they threw in the market in an effort to bid up the value of the American currency."[6] In Friedman's view, this was like trying to calm a starved gorilla by offering it a raisin for lunch and, of course, the effort had little or no effect on the market.

> Whose world is this anyway? The answer is that it is increasingly Adam Smith's world—a world in which the balance of power between global financial markets and governments is tilting toward markets ... Twenty-two-year-old bond traders with ice water for blood tyrannize the President, passing judgment on his economic performance by raising or lowering interest rates; the markets devour central bank cash with nary a burp, and the portfolio managers, playing global Monopoly, move cash from country to country, deciding which governments deserve to "Pass Go" and collect $200 billion and which should go directly to jail and be starved of the capital to raise living standards.[7]

The effect of the global money market on economic policy decisions of supposedly sovereign nation-states is best summarized by Lowell Bryan, a director (senior partner) of McKinsey & Company, one of the world's leading business consulting firms, who heads the firm's North American Financial Institutions practice.

His new view of the nature and function of the international financial market might be summarized as follows. We still tend to think about financial markets largely in national terms because, until recently, the instruments of investment, the prices, and the risks have varied so widely from country to country. We are conditioned to think about global integration in terms of trade flows even though the world's economy is increasingly being driven by capital flows. Most people in each nation believe that their respective national governments still have complete control over their own local financial economy. In fact, they have lost much of their ability to control exchange rates and interest rates, and they are gradually losing control over the financial institutions they regulate. [8]

At this point, the reader might well ask how does this relate to the main subject we are dealing with, the future of work and wealth in the American economy?

This parenthetical chapter on money markets is included to show their relationship to national policy making, particularly as regards social expenditures, which many experts feel should be considerably increased to confront problems facing the U.S. as we move from an industrial to a post-industrial, or information age, economy.

Bryan and co-author Diana Farrell point out that the political pressures on the leaders of national governments to increase social expenditures, which soon become viewed as entitlements, are enormous. Barring any unusual increase in productivity and wealth, the only solutions open to governments to fund these expenditures are large hikes in taxes, printing more money or borrowing. Tax increases are unpopular and may hurt the economy by taking investment capital and spending capacities out of the system, printing more money leads to inflation and currency devaluation; therefore the usual recourse of governments is to increase borrowing, especially abroad. Many countries soon reach their limits of credit-worthiness in the international money markets and are forced to cut back on their social expenditures in order to avoid a credit or currency crisis. This means cutting the very entitlements for which borrowing was undertaken: pensions, health care, unemployment and social welfare that make up the vast majority of spending. This causes further trauma, not only to the economy of a given country but to its political and social structures as well. Yet, various authors cited in this chapter insist that the new realities of the global capital market are such that sooner or later all countries, even the United States, will be obliged to follow this route. Bryan and Farrell agree that the only question is whether these nations cut voluntarily or are forced to do so by a market crisis. Either way, the market will curtail consumption making more capital available globally for investment.

In short, one of the historic provinces of each nation-state—to regulate, to print money, to tax, to subsidize and to borrow money largely without constraint—is fast becoming a dead letter; the capital markets will constrain what governments can do not the other way around.

It is this growing dilemma between what is necessary to cushion the transition from the old industrial age society to the new era dominated by information age technology on one hand and the ability of governments to finance such initiatives on the other that forms the central core of this book. Unfortunately, there are no pat answers to this major dilemma, nor do I share the view of the so-called optimists that there are no major transition problems to be solved. The solutions—if there are any—to this apparent policy impasse will have to be worked out over time by many policy makers. But before any solutions can be developed, there must be general awareness that the problems exist and will not go away.

Chapter 5

America in Decline?

In previous chapters I have mentioned a central dilemma which the U.S. and other industrialized countries face as the world enters an era of transformational change similar to that of the Industrial Revolution in the 18th and 19th centuries. This dilemma is related to the growing need for measures to cushion the economic and social effects of radical change versus the diminishing ability of sovereign states to unilaterally finance such remedies, given the increasingly independent and inherently conservative nature of global capital markets. The traditional way for governments to finance programs—such as those mentioned in Chapter 2, which are aimed at alleviating the pain of change— is to borrow funds and/or to print more money. Both of these methods are now subject to the independent scrutiny and control of organizations and individuals who owe no allegiance to the country in question. The other major way to finance such operations is through economic growth. Increase the national wealth and there should be resources sufficient to fund the necessary welfare and work programs. The question then arises as to the ability of any country's economy to undertake such growth.

The world-famous economist Robert Heilbroner, makes a distinction between "normal" economic growth and "transformational" growth. By "normal" growth, he refers to the expansive properties of the capitalist system when businesses are pursuing their interests as best they can without the stimulus of a visibly expanding production frontier. Growth of this kind typically fails to offer full employment; therefore, most contemporary states use techniques derived from Keynesian economic theory to "fine tune" their economies in order to reach adequate employment levels and assist national welfare. In Heilbroner's view, "transformational" growth is another matter. This condition emerges when the production frontier is dramatically extended, usually by the technological advances that open vast new investment possibilities, such as the expansion of the railroads in the 19th century or the development of the automobile in the 20th. As Heilbroner states: "Such booms are highly employment generating, but they come irregularly, and we do not know how to create them in their absence. Thus, whereas it is imaginable that new transformational changes will provide the system with its needed impetus during the coming century, it would be foolhardy in the extreme to count on such a fortuitous turn of affairs. Indeed...the current trend in technological advance points in a much less comforting direction."[1] But current technological change may not carry long-term expansive consequences for employment. Like the social critics mentioned in Chapter 2, Heilbroner considers the possibility of a reduction in the need for labor comparable to that which has halved the number of manufacturing jobs in seventy years along with a substantial reduction in the supervisory tasks associated with middle management. The more intense the efforts of any one country to pursue full employment policies to correct this situation, the more likely it is that inflationary wage pressures will be generated. Given the ease with which enterprises can shift their operations elsewhere, these pressures will increase the movement of capital to countries that tolerate unemployment and enjoy a lower inflation rate. In addition, the fiscal burdens of maintaining high employment will drive industries and capital to less heavily taxing countries. Therefore, in Heilbroner's view, it seems difficult in a globalized world economy, for any country, on its own, to institute an effective, long-run pro-employment policy. At the same time, the prospects seem dim for international agreements to dampen the movement of capital to avoid this beggar-thy-neighbor quandary. Indeed, the time may already have passed when any nation-state or combination of nation-states can contain the unfettered movement of capital funds around the globe. Heilbroner's <u>Visions of the Future</u>, is a wide-ranging analysis of the political economy of societies from earliest civilizations to the present day, with speculation on the prospects of the capitalist system in the 21st century. He abjures speculating on the course of events over an extended period of time in the future, but ventures the belief that a system of various types of capitalism is the most probable political setting for the Western world in the next century. He also believes that ultimately capitalism will exhaust its vitality, making way in some countries for a more egalitarian society and in others for more centralization and control.

Heilbroner offers two very different visions of the economic future in the capitalist world. The first is a gradual worsening of economic performance brought about by rising levels of technological unemployment. He refuses to speculate on the socio-political outcome of such deterioration, but considers the prospect anxiety provoking. The second plausible outcome points to a vision of a "more pragmatic and concerned capitalism" (presumably with a heavy mix of socialism), following policies similar to those mentioned in Chapter 2. However, this will probably require the creation of an international agreement to protect the nations who adopt such policies against destructive flights of capital, and the prospects for such agreements are uncertain. At the same time, his prognosis for the achievement of a transition to a social-democratic capitalism modeled on the Swedish economy for countries such as the United States is not promising; it is difficult to see how the political will necessary for such an effort could be brought into being, "especially in a country that has adopted the cowboy as its national social hero." As a consequence, the future of the U.S. economy is not promising: "(E)ven though capitalism is today a social order without external challenge, military or political, it seems difficult to imagine that it will easily resolve the economic problems that spring from its nature and hover over its future."[2] Heilbroner's hope for the United States is a summoning of national political will comparable to that which built the Panama Canal and brought into being the New Deal, to initiate a new kind of publicly led transformational boom of unspecified nature. Failing this, he foresees that the capitalist democracies will probably steer a conservative and cautious rather than a radical and bold course, but that politics of caution will not be sufficient to alleviate the strains and dysfunctions that the country faces.

Other analysts of stature and prestige have forecast a similarly gloomy and anxiety-filled future for American society. A leader of this declinist group is Jeffrey Madrick, an Emmy Award-winning economics reporter for NBC and editor of Challenge, who explains why prosperity has eluded so many Americans and why, since the early 1970s and until recently, America's rate of economic growth has declined dramatically, bringing with it a whole series of political and social problems. His prognosis for the future is, like Heilbroner's, filled with foreboding. Unlike Heilbroner, he believes that there may be no overall solution to slow economic growth in the U.S. and ends his analysis on the following gloomy note:

> Until we acknowledge the fundamental change in our circumstances, see that our problems are not primarily moral and ideological, and reduce our fear of a world in which we can no longer count on constant rapid material gain, we cannot begin to seek workable solutions. We may ultimately abandon our most cherished political convictions, and this would be a disaster. Throughout our history we believed that we were a chosen people, a belief essentially sustained by our growing affluence. Now we shall see who we are without it. [3]

In arriving at this downbeat vision of America's economic future, Madrick discusses and dismisses the solutions to slow economic growth put forth by many experts. In his opinion, none of the suggested remedies will work anymore—increasing the flexibility and competitiveness of our businesses, raising our savings rate, balancing the budget, improving our education, and developing new markets for our goods overseas—all are rendered ineffectual by the dynamics of the new high-tech global marketplace. Our faith that technological progress will inevitably sustain fast growth is no longer warranted.

It may be appropriate to cite the reasons for Madrick's skepticism regarding the promise of technology for economic growth. He reminds us that scientific and technological breakthroughs have always gone hand-in-hand with rapid economic growth in the U.S., hence it would be logical to assume that in the future everything from robotics to biotechnology, personal computers, interactive telecommunications and the so-called information highway will provide the second coming of a miraculous breakthrough, like the railroads, the car, and electricity in the past. However, he warns that the real test of technological breakthroughs is how well an economy can exploit them: for example, the railroads were important to American economic development, but not as important as the mass market they helped to create, which in turn stimulated the construction of still more railroads. Madrick then notes that under current conditions many countries now share the advantageous economic environment that the U.S. once shared with few other countries. Today no nation can count on holding the lead indefinitely in new production technologies and management practices; the new technologies which underlie many of the fastest-growing industries are increasingly scientifically based, making them inherently more subject to competition than the older, largely mechanical production technologies, which depended on hands-on experience and the advantages of scale conferred by a large marketplace. Highly trained scientists and technicians everywhere are increasingly able to translate the latest technological advances into an industrial advantage in their own countries, often at relatively low labor and production costs. At the same time, countries such as Japan have penetrated the high-technology industries and are capturing world-wide market shares. Science and technology will surely continue to advance around the world, but it is a mistake to assume that the U.S. economy will automatically benefit from the new technologies to the degree it once did, especially if our economy continues to grow slowly: technological breakthroughs, no matter how large, no longer automatically confer even semi-permanent leads on those who make them. The competition is now ongoing and intense, returns are short-lived, and outcomes more uncertain.

At the same time, Madrick states that modern production techniques—such as flexible production and distribution which some experts believe will provide new stimulus for America's competitiveness or will make the U.S. economy more productive—have not yet produced the gigantic gains in productivity that mass production provided when it was first adopted. Similarly, new marketing and distribution techniques in traditional services have not compensated entirely for the cost of servicing fragmented markets. As a result, the growth in productivity in services remains much slower than it once was. In the twenty years that flexible production has been widely adopted in the advanced world, the rate of productive growth in the sixteen richest nations fell on average by nearly half, to 2.3 percent a year since the early 1970s, compared with 4.5 percent a year between the end of World II and 1973. Finally, there is no guarantee that American business will be as good at flexible production as our international rivals. As a consequence, to assume a productivity revolution in this country caused by the new technologies similar to that which occurred earlier in this century "requires a leap of faith that our economic experience doesn't yet justify."[4]

Madrick's pessimistic view of the future of the American economy and of U.S. society in general is typical of a number of highly regarded social critics and merits further comment. In this author's opinion, Madrick's observations on decline fall into two categories. The first has to do with the fact that the make-up of the current global economy and the nature of late 20th century scientific and technology breakthroughs no longer confer the automatic advantages that America, with its huge and prosperous continental market and leads in production, marketing and distribution techniques, enjoyed in the immediate post World War II era and earlier in the century. By the same token, no other country on the planet has a lock on the global marketplace and many cannot compete with the U.S. in terms of its large domestic market, its educated, highly mobile work force attuned to change, nor with this country's experienced management teams and truly world class university and research facilities. Furthermore, the U.S. financial system, having already undergone a series of necessary reforms and technological upgrading, is solid and operating with state-of-the-art techniques. Also, the dollar is still the world's reserve currency and the currency most used in world trade. The strength of the dollar in trade and finance is a reflection of the confidence of the world's bankers in the fundamental strength and future prospects of the U.S. economy.

This does not suggest that the U.S. enjoys an impregnable and commanding lead in the global economy—no one country enjoys such advantages—but the U.S. can and does compete with the best of them. Furthermore, the U.S. leads the world in basic scientific breakthroughs, and this lead will most likely continue for the foreseeable future. As a result, the U.S. is in a strong position to continue to compete and to maintain a substantial share of the world market: as the global economy grows, the U.S. should more than share in this growth.

The other main observation on America's decline by Jeffrey Madrick requires more lengthy treatment; and several comments are in order. Economist Lester Thurow recently observed that economic models are good at describing fundamental forces and pressures, but they are of little use when it comes to timing. Consequently, to say that empirical evidence does not lead to the conclusion that productivity increases will soon come from the new technology and that to believe so requires a leap of faith is simply to say that nobody can be sure when or to what extent such increases in productivity will occur. Other experts consider that such large productivity increases are on the horizon (or may already have begun to arrive), and that they will be substantial and long-lasting, as I will shortly argue. Furthermore, there is ample empirical evidence to document the fact that similar productivity increases have occurred in the past as a result of technological advances. This phenomenon was substantiated in a recent study prepared by Professor Jeremy Greenwood for the American Enterprise Institute. Greenwood points out that the adoption of new technologies is notoriously slow; there is a lag between the introduction of new technologies and the advance of labor productivity. This lag is often accompanied by a short run surge in wage inequality since educated, skilled workers adapt more easily to the new technologies than the unskilled ones. According to Dr. Greenwood: "At the dawn of an industrial revolution, the long-run advance in labor productivity temporarily pauses as economic agents undertake the (unmeasured) investment in information required to get new technologies operating closer to their full potential". [5]

Some experts believe that this adaptation pause in U.S. economic growth has already occurred and is drawing to a close. Robert Samuelson recently stated that the American economy is stronger now than it has been in many years: this country produces more than twice as much as its next largest competitor (Japan), is 15-to-20 percent more efficient per worker, remains the world's largest exporter and retains leadership in many critical technologies. More importantly, productivity gains are accelerating. After averaging about 1 percent annually in the 1970s and 1980s – well below the 3 percent average of the 1950s and 1960s – gains have risen and as recently as March 1998 were in the range of 2.25 percent. [6]

In the case of earlier technological revolutions, productivity lags lasted decades rather than a few years. But it is possible to argue that under present conditions in the new global high-tech economy such lags will be considerably shortened and, furthermore, the overall economic growth caused by innovative change could last over a long period of time rather than coming in relatively short bursts as in the past.

In all fairness to Jeff Madrick and to other experts who do not subscribe to the rosy scenarios described in greater detail in the next chapter, the jury is still out as regards the possible revolutionary effects on the U.S. economy of the wide-spread use of computers. In a recent article, Madrick correctly points out that there is no empirical evidence as yet to sustain the belief that a rate of growth of more than 2.5 percent can be sustained for a long period of time. Citing a recent study by the Brookings

Institution that attempts to estimate the likely contributions of computers to the economy's productivity under several hypotheses, he concludes that under the more optimistic assumptions regarding computer returns on investment the contribution of the computer revolution to growth is no more than 0.61 percent a year, and 0.51 percent after depreciation. This is significant but not adequate to put the economy back on its former fast track. [7]

This report will not constitute the last word in this important on-going debate on the economic effects of new technology. For example, Madrick points out that information technology yields what economists call "social" returns, i.e., financial advantages that accrue even to those businesses which don't invest in computers. These social returns may yet surprise us, and more precise methods of measuring the size of investments will probably be found. Other economic studies currently underway may shed new light on this matter, not just in the context of the effect of computers but of other advanced technologies as well. The fact remains that empirical evidence is currently insufficient to prove or disprove any forecast of the economic effects of the new technologies. Therefore, any view of the future of the American economy involves a large element of faith in one vision or the other: only time will tell which vision is correct.

Let us turn now to the views of those who see a long boom for the American economy, lasting some decades into the future.

Chapter 6

The Long Boom

Chapter 3 stated that five waves of technology—computers, telecommunications, biotechnology, nanotechnology, and alternative energy—will bring big productivity increases that should lead to high rates of economic growth in the next decades. This chapter will review of some the reasons for this optimistic view of the future of the American economy.

At the outset, it should be mentioned that these optimistic forecasts are based on the following set of basic assumptions:

(1) That technological changes cited below will develop at overall accelerated rates, observe general continuity over an extended period of time, have wide-ranging effects on the economies of individual countries, and enjoy a basic similarity between countries. These assumptions of the effects of modern technological developments on economic growth are based on the historical experience of the last two centuries.[1]

(2) The second set of assumptions is more controversial and are based on the belief that knowledge and ideas have become vital engines of economic growth, following the concepts of New Growth Theory of economist Paul Romer and others. Knowledge, in this context, entails taking objects that are relatively worthless and rearranging them into new combinations to create value (as sand, which has little value, can be turned into a computer chip which becomes immensely valuable). It also involves reorganizing processes and organizations to make them more efficient and faster acting. Some observers consider that information or knowledge is now a major factor of production, along with the traditional factors: land, labor and capital. Although these other factors are, to some extent, fixed and finite in nature, knowledge is inexhaustible, infinitely expandable and highly mobile. Walter Wriston, former Chairman of Citicorp, notes that the Information Revolution is rapidly creating new wealth, the source of which is not material: it is information,

knowledge applied to work to create value. The information technologies are forging a new economy, as different from the industrial economy as the industrial was from the agricultural. Technological gains are spread throughout this new economy, and their pace and intensity of growth are without historical precedent. [2]

At the same time, other writers, including Richard Easterlin in his recent historical analysis of economic growth in the last 200 years—have observed that modern economic progress has consistently had as a principal basis the application of new technologies to the production and distribution of goods and services.

> During the course of the eighteenth century in Great Britain, there was a marked upsurge in the rate and scope of invention, which has traditionally been termed the first Industrial Revolution. Inventions in steam power and wrought iron laid the basis for the gradual emergence of a new general purpose technology applicable in sector after sector throughout the economy - from manufacturing, transportation and communications to agriculture and construction. Toward the end of the nineteenth century new inventions in power and materials gave birth to a second Industrial Revolution, another general purpose technology based on electricity, the internal combustion engine, steel, non-ferrous metals and plastics. Like the first, the second Industrial Revolution gradually transformed methods of production in industry after industry. [3]

These industrial revolutions have wrought economic transformations unprecedented in human history. Statistics indicate that among the principal industrialized countries, real output per capita (productivity) has grown at an unprecedented rate - averaging about 20 percent per decade since 1820. [4]

Easterlin believes that the world is embarked on a new process of irreversible economic growth, a post-industrial or third Industrial Revolution rooted in breakthroughs in human knowledge. In his view, this growth should be widespread throughout the world in the 21st century, not just in those countries already at the technological frontier. For the developed countries such as the U.S., he predicts a continued long-term up trend in per capita income through at least the middle of the 21st century. This growth should result in cheaper and higher quality goods and services for the general public, help create high-paying jobs in new areas of economic life and raise the standard of living of the population as a whole.

As pointed out in previous chapters, these rosy scenarios of future prosperity and growth are often attacked by many experts as wishful thinking. However, there is a growing body of observers, including this writer, who champion the concept of a long-term economic boom in the U.S. and other countries, fueled by the scientific and technological breakthroughs of the late 20th and early 21st century.

In order to substantiate this belief, it is appropriate to briefly review the nature of these scientific and technological developments and their potential for economic growth.

Computers and Telecommunications

Much has been written about the revolutionary effects on society of computers and their handmaiden, global telecommunications. The modern computer, an offshoot of World War II's defense effort, has already transformed society in the developed world and will continue to do so for many decades to come. David reminds us that the engine driving this ongoing revolution is the microprocessor, the heart of the computer which for some 20 years has doubled in speed on the average of every 18 months.[5] This new technology has led to countless inventions, such as portable computers and fax machines, and has added intelligence to many devices such as automobiles and wrist watches. Microprocessors' performance has improved 25,000 times over since their invention only 25 years ago, and many industries simply could no longer function without their use; for example, airlines and financial service firms are often forced to slow down or stop operations when their computers go down. This exponential growth in productivity, coupled with steadily decreasing costs in computer equipment, will probably continue for some time. Microsoft Chairman Bill Gates predicts that this increase in computing power, known as Moore's Law, will continue for at least 20 years, by which time a computation which now takes a day will be more than 10,000 times faster and thus take fewer than 10 seconds![6]

The rapid growth of telecommunications follows a similar upward curve. The breakup of Ma Bell, initiated in 1982, triggered a frenzy of entrepreneurial activity as nascent companies like MCI and Sprint raced to build fiber optic networks across the country. By the early 1990's, these companies shifted from moving voice to moving data as a new phenomenon seemed to come out of nowhere: the Internet. Computers and communications became inextricably linked, each feeding the phenomenal growth of the other. By the late 1990's, the telecom went wireless. Mobile phone systems and all-purpose personal communications services arrived first, with vast antennae networks on the ground. Soon after, big satellite projects came on-line. By 1998, the Iridium global phone network was complete. It is predicted that by 2002, Teledesic's global Internet network will be operational. These projects, among others, allow seamless connection to the information infrastructure anywhere on the planet by early in the next century. By 2005, high band-width connections that can easily move video will have become common in developed countries, and videophones will finally catch on.[7]

This symbiotic relationship between computer and communications technology is leading to a major economic discontinuity generally attributed to the explosive growth of the Internet. New forms of on-line commerce are springing up as well as more efficient and speedier methods of product distribution.

On the production side, a number of books have described the revolutionary effects of computer-assisted design and manufacturing techniques, most notably Shosana Zuboff's <u>In the Age of the Smart Machine</u>. These technologies are also spurring the reorganization of businesses as well as institutions outside the business world: all the way from hospitals and educational institutions to lawyers' offices and the courts as well as municipal, state and federal government operations. (These reorganization efforts are leading to dramatic improvements in efficiency and productivity, although not without human toll, a thorough discussion of this topic can be found in management guru Peter Drucker's recent books: <u>The New Realities</u> and <u>Managing in a Time of Great Change</u>.)

Until recently, these technological miracles have not had a marked effect on official productivity statistics. However, there is a growing body of evidence that the long awaited productivity payoffs from information technology are finally beginning to appear. Growth in non-farm business productivity, which limped along at 1 percent per year during the 1980s, topped 5 percent in the last half of 1993 and has averaged close to 2 percent over the last few years. Manufacturing productivity has been rising at a 3.8 percent annual clip since 1991, a threefold increase over rates in the 1970s and 1980s. These increases are finally showing up in overall productivity growth which increased by 2.25 percent in 1997.[8] These productivity increases add value to the economy and are a major key to sustained economic growth. Just how sustained and how high this rate of growth will be is a matter of speculation among professional futurists. <u>Wired</u> Magazine projected that the real growth rate in the world's domestic product will rise from the 3% to 4% range it has averaged in the last decades to hit an astounding 6% in 2005: continued growth at this rate will double the size of the world economy in just 12 years, doubling it twice in 25 years. This level of growth would surpass the rates of the last global economic boom, which averaged 4.9% from 1950 to 1973.[9] The well-known futurist Joseph Coates assumes a more modest rate of increase: Gross Domestic Product (GDP) growth on a <u>per</u>

capita basis of about 2 to 2.5% over the next 30 years. Even under this more conservative assumption, per capita income in the U.S. would double from 1995 to 2025.[10] A long-term growth forecast in the 3 to 4% range appears to this writer to be more in line with past growth patterns during times of economic expansion.

Many futurists do not base their optimistic forecasts of economic growth on the effects of computer and communications technology alone. Nevertheless, these observers are convinced that the current surge of technological change is a major contributor to said growth and that it differs from anything seen before for two major reasons. One is the exponential increase in computing power, growing at an unprecedented rate, roughly doubling in performance every 18 months or so. The other is the rapid spread of this technology, which is beginning to affect every area of contemporary life. As an article in the Wall Street Journal puts it: "No technology has ever been so protean, so unrestrained by physical limits, so capable of cutting large swaths through unrelated industries such as banking, power utilities, insurance and telecommunications." [11] The authors of this article could have added that no technology in the past has attained so rapidly a global reach, so much so that some now talk about the birth of a world-wide networked economy in which every facet of human activity is transformed in some way by the emergent fabric of interconnection. Such visions of a new economy may be fanciful and the ultimate consequences of these changes may be impossible to foresee at this time, but most observers agree that they will surely be far reaching.

Biotechnology

Computers and telecommunications are not the only new technologies that have the potential for transforming society. Another area that has a similar potential is biotechnology, an umbrella term that covers various techniques for using the properties of living things to make products or provide services. Biotechnology, like computer technology, has a long series of antecedents dating back to the 17th century but really came into its own with the discovery of the structure of DNA by James Watson and Francis Crick in 1953. DNA (deoxyribonucleic acid) is the material from which genes are made and genes, in turn, are the physical unit of inheritance. By manipulating the genetic code, scientists can change the properties of living things, can alter organisms in very specific ways.

In many respects, the genetic code and DNA—the storage vehicle for genetic information—can be considered the "little black box" that directs what each living thing is to become. For those interested in a complete description of this powerful new tool which is revolutionizing medicine, agriculture and other areas of our lives, a number of books can be consulted, particularly Eric Grace's book <u>Biotechnology Unzipped,</u> [12] but for the purposes of this work, suffice it to mention some of the many applications, both actual and potential, of biotechnology. Since economists still cannot agree on ways to measure all the benefits and costs of this type of technology, it is premature to attempt to quantify its possible effects on productivity and other economic benchmarks, but most observers will agree that the actual and potential benefits to mankind to be derived from biotechnology are enormous. Following are a few of the products and services, actual or potential, to be derived from biotechnology, as discussed in Eric Grace's book.

Human health care

- Organ transplants with matching tissues that will not be rejected by the patient's body.

- New biomaterials and body parts grown from scratch.

- Diagnosis and cure of illness as through gene therapy, often involving previously incurable diseases.

- Commercial production of drugs through genetic engineering, often involving chemicals that might be diffi-

cult and costly to extract or simply unavailable by conventional means.

- Design of new drugs custom-made for specific purposes
  using computer technology.

- A great step forward is the ongoing Human Genome
  Project scheduled to be completed by 2005. This is an
  international research effort to map and sequence all
  100,000 or so genes found in human DNA, which in
  turn, will make possible the development of all sorts of
  treatments to avoid or hinder diseases.

Applications in agriculture

- Increasing plant yields, using biotechnology to develop
  plants that survive environmental stresses, resist pests
  and diseases, tolerate herbicides and grow in poor
  soils.

- Developing crops that have less need for artificial fer-
  tilizers and have a longer shelf life, higher nutritional
  content, etc.

- Producing healthier and faster-growing livestock with
  higher quality meat, eggs, etc.

- Developing vaccines, diagnoses and disease-resistance
  for farm animals along with higher reproductive potential.

- Turning plants and animals into living factories for
  making drugs, industrial chemicals, fuels, plastics,
  medical products including organs for humans, and
  other materials.

Other applications

- Using environmental biotechnology to develop processes and products that clean up pollution, monitor environmental health and produce energy and materials in less destructive ways.

- Creating new techniques and products from the vast untapped well of living resources found in the seas and natural forests, including new materials, medicines, chemicals and fuels.

Other Advanced Technologies

Until recently, the following scientific developments belonged in the category of science fiction but are now being seriously discussed as bright new technologies of the 21st century: nanotechnology, alternative energy sources, high-temperature superconductors, intelligent materials, etc.

Nanotechnology

This new technology involves manufacturing by manipulating atoms or molecules directly or through chemical and biological means, using enzymes, proteins, and imitations of biochemical processes for making customized materials designed for highly specific functions, such as biological computer chips, molecular switches and molecular magnets. The goal is to build devices from the bottom up, atom by atom. This would theoretically make products cheaper, stronger, lighter, more efficient and more reliable. [13]

Alternative energy sources[14]

Modern economies are critically dependent on energy to power farms, factories, homes and offices. As traditional energy sources become depleted and hence more expensive to exploit, new sources of energy must be developed along with new methods of reducing energy use. A number of solutions to the energy problem exist and are projected to enter into widespread use in the next decades. These include:

- Hybrid electric cars
- Hydrogen cars based on gasoline
- Hybrid cars fueled by pure hydrogen
- Use of super strong, ultra light materials that take the place of steel and allow big savings on mileage.

In addition, a number of experts predict that these alternatives to fossil fuels will become commercially viable and be increasingly utilized:

- Intensive use of solar energy and wind power, including vastly improved methods of storing energy.

- Energy derived from atomic fusion.

- High-temperature super conductors that could greatly increase efficient generation, transmission and storage of electricity.

To sum up: the above-mentioned areas of technological break throughs have the potential of bringing about productivity increases that could, in the coming decades, lead to high rates of economic growth and the creation of substantial new wealth. This in turn, could be used to solve many of the social problems cited in Chapter 2, as well as other difficulties facing society. But, there is no guarantee that such events will occur or, if they occur, that the increased wealth will be wisely spent. However, there is reason to believe in a brighter future, though the optimistic vision is tempered with the conviction that the transition to a new Information Age economy will not be easy. There is potential for a tremendous amount of trauma in this process and pressure on all of us to adjust to the wrenching changes in our lives. The nature of some of these changes and the possible responses to them will be the subject of the next chapters.

Chapter 7

A Time of Great Abundance

The last two chapters were devoted to presenting various views of the future of the American economy. On the darker side of the visions of such experts as Robert Heilbroner and Jeffrey Madick depict a country in deep trouble brought about by rising unemployment due to technological change, inability to compete in the global marketplace and a host of other ills—all of which appear incurable barring a radical change in our capitalist system. On the brighter side, we have the views of such techno-optimists as Walter Wriston, Bill Gates and Michael Moynihan who predict an American economic renaissance spurred by new computer and communications systems and other technological breakthroughs currently on the drawing boards.

It would seem that there is no way to reconcile these two very different visions of the future and yet, based on many years of working with and contemplating problems of socio-economic change, I hold that both sets of views are partially correct and are describing the same phenomenon of change. In this respect, I agree with many observers in believing that the U.S. and the rest of the world is going through a transition period as extensive and as wrenching as Industrial Revolution; only this new revolutionary period of change is enormously compressed in time. The so-called Industrial Revolution took some 200 years to run its course; the post-Industrial, high-tech Revolution began some 40 years ago and its effects are now being felt throughout the globe. Although its final outcome is unclear, the disturbing effects of change during the transition period of this new Revolution are now being felt. The result is a divided and simultaneous impression of progress and decline: rise of the new order, fall of the old. If this view of the transition period is correct, then it will be difficult to reach a synthesis of opinions on the future: it is the best of times and the worst of times and the long-term outcome is in doubt.

On the other hand, the purpose of this book is to discuss the long-term prospects of work and wealth in 21st century America, and one way to deal with this very complex situation is to do what many futurists attempt: to engage in informed speculation on outcomes and produce scenarios or visions of things to come using a time horizon of some 30 to 40 years into the future.

Many futurists in recent years purport to do just that. An international organization, The World Future Society, which brings out a number of publications and sponsors seminars and conferences on future-related subjects every year; a few universities such as The University of Houston and The University of Hawaii, have centers for future studies. I have included in the References at the end of this book some of the current publications in this field and can especially recommend to the general reader the book written by Joseph Coates, John Mahaffie and Andy Hines entitled 2025: Scenarios of US and Global Society, Reshaped by Science and Technology. This book constitutes, in my view, one of the best attempts at predicting what American society will look like some 30 years from now. Written from the historical perspective, it contains a set of 15 scenarios of the world in 2025, covering trends in medicine, housing, agriculture, industry, education, ecology and other key aspects of society in the United States as well as other countries. Not surprisingly, the book has a basically positive outlook, at least for the so-called advanced industrialized nations, starting with the assumption that people and organizations are capable of using emerging science and technological capabilities in ways that will be useful, profitable, and of benefit to humanity over the next generation.

My own views of the future of U.S. society are limited to the two areas: wealth and work in the 21st century, during the next 30 years or so. With regard to wealth—or rather the possible future growth of the American economy—I agree with the experts cited in the last chapter that the U.S. economy is entering a period of unprecedented and sustained growth that should do much to alleviate, if not to solve, some of our seemingly intractable problems like poverty and to ease tensions throughout the world. Although I do not subscribe to the relentlessly optimistic viewpoint of the authors of the previously cited article, "The Long Boom", I do agree with their belief that some of the forces that caused high rates of growth in the 1950s and 1960s may be echoed in strikingly similar, if not still more powerful, forces in motion today. The "Long Boom" writers argue:

> The end of the military state of readiness in the 1880s, as in the 1940s, unleashed an array of new technologies, not the least of which is the Internet. The end of the Cold War also saw the triumph of a set of ideas long championed in the United States. Those of the free market economy and, to some extent, liberal democracy. This cleared the way for the creation of a truly global economy, one integrated market. Not one large colonial empire. Everybody in the planet in the same economy. This is historically unprecedented, with unprecedented consequences to follow.[1]

I might add that another historically unprecedented event is the exponential growth of scientific and mechanical knowledge, a non-material and potentially inexhaustible resource which has become a major factor of production and productivity. Although the concept of knowledge applied to work to create value as a major source of new wealth is still controversial, and sufficient empirical evidence is not yet at hand to prove its validity (perhaps because today's methods of calculating the gross national product fail, except indirectly, to capture the benefits of rapidly accumulating knowledge, as Walter Wriston points out), Nevertheless, I cannot fail to be impressed with the growing body of scientific and technological breakthroughs that, if history is any guide, should lead to increased wealth. As Wriston also notes, at least 80 percent of all of the scientists who ever lived are now alive! At least half of all scientific research in the US has been conducted in the last two decades, leading to a doubling of the total stock of scientific and technological knowledge about every ten to twelve years. Staid economists still hesitate to announce the advent of a new Information Age economy, but futurists, myself included, do not hesitate to herald this event. Furthermore, futurists also venture to forecast significant rates of increase in the national economy, ranging from a conservative annual average of 2% over the next two or three decades to an astounding 6% starting early in the next century. I personally favor the view that the US gross national product will continue the present trend and grow at an average rate of between 3 and 4%. If this is true, we might see a doubling of real per capita income in the U.S. in some 20 years, which could generate sufficient revenues to deal with many of our accumulated problems as well as invest in new initiatives, such as those outlined in Chapter 2, to cushion the transition to the new Information Age.

Admittedly, this positive vision for America assumes many unproven things, not the least of which is that the large increase in wealth would generate sufficient tax revenues to deal with national needs and that these resources would be wisely spent—large assumptions indeed! Nevertheless, as one who has spent most of his working career in promoting economic and social development in Third World countries, I believe similar development possible for the U.S. and other "advanced" nations in transition to a post-industrial society.

The subject of the future of work in the U.S. requires greater elaboration and can be divided into two different categories: one refers to the prospects for Information Age workers—the symbolic analysts, to use Robert Reich's term; the other refers to other groups – some 60 to 80% of the work force – who do not qualify as symbolic analysts. Related to this is the question of the future of workers' organizations—union and non-union—which also merit a few comments.

As mentioned in Chapter 2, the so-called symbolic analysts' jobs include professionals such as doctors and lawyers and computer experts, workers in "creative" fields such as writers and artists, and, finally, top management jobs in the corporate world. The outlook for such workers is generally bright and any number of books and articles have come out recently giving advice to these lucky people on how to best position themselves to get the maximum out of their privileged positions in society.[2]   These publications can be obtained from the World Future Society and will not be summarized here; there is, however, a common thread running through all this advice to symbolic analysts:

(a) Be prepared to switch jobs and relocate with increasing frequency. A corollary of this is the idea that loyalty to your employer is no longer as important as loyalty to one's career field, networking is vital to learn of new job opportunities and to keep abreast of new developments in your area of specialization.

(b) Be prepared for change by taking every opportunity to expand skills and knowledge that is transferable to new work situations. This involves lifelong education and development, not just formal education but retraining, attendance at work-shops and seminars, reading current books and articles, etc. Bright employment prospects do not assure success for each and every worker, and as always, the burden of success falls on the individual. Those who are best prepared to meet the challenges of the job market will reap the benefits, others may fall by the wayside; but, by and large, the chances of success are good for all symbolic analysts.

What is of real concern, at least to this writer, is the fate of those who do not fall into this elite category of Information Age workers. The "non-symbolic analyst" category is a large one, comprising what many experts believe will reach some 80% of the entire work force, including routine production jobs, the tra-ditional blue collar workers of industrial America—a vanishing breed—to jobs in the in-person server category such as retail sales personnel, waiters, hospital attendants, etc. The conven-tional forecast for these persons—the vast majority of the workforce—is not encouraging. Many experts, including those cited in Chapter 2, foresee not only a vast gap between the pay scales of privileged information workers and the others but something even more ominous: a polarization of workers into "elite" and "non-elite" strata, depending on their educational background. A recent study whose findings confirm that well-paid, relatively satisfying jobs are being created in the "new" economy – 33% of workers between 30 and 59 now hold "elite" jobs, compared to only 28% in 1979. The average pay for these jobs had risen over the period of this study to $47,000, though it has fallen in recent years. But, more significantly, there is growing evidence of a fundamental polarization of workers into what some observers call "the two-tiered" economy—a growing gap between America's two levels of workers. "While a higher proportion than before are doing well, the remaining two-thirds of US workers have either middle-income jobs, which pay on the average $29,000 a year, or low-income jobs which pay an average of $19,000 a year. By contrast with the elite workers, the average income for both of these groups has fallen significantly since 1979... the most telling portrait yet of a divided America in the 1990's." [3]

Some writers of a more pessimistic bent project this polarization trend far into the future. One writer talks of the "Brazilianization" of the United States, referring to that South American country where only a small proportion of the population has high incomes and well-paying jobs and the vast majority live in poverty and ignorance, with little hope of bettering their lot in life.

Is this, truly, the fate of workers in the U.S. and other advanced industrialized countries? Will Information Age technology bring, not social progress, but a regression to life as it was lived in earlier centuries, and as it is still lived in most parts of the so-called Third World? What a cruelly ironic situation it would be if the successful exploitation of scientific breakthroughs should lead only to the degradation of the U.S. to the status of an underdeveloped country!

Writers of a more optimistic bent tend to downplay the differences in pay scales of information workers and others and emphasize the new employment opportunities that are being created in the "new" economy. Few actually deal directly with the subject of the long-term prospects in the 21st century for those who, for whatever reason, are not able to join the ranks of the symbolic analysts.

A few far-sighted commentators confront this situation.

Peter Drucker, Joseph Coates and others have stressed the increasing role in the U.S. economy of the Third Sector, or non-profit organizations, distinct from government and business. Drucker points out that the role of the Third Sector in the economy has been to deal with activities that seem inappropriate for government and that do not find a ready business market. These organizations, which include the American Red Cross as well as the local settlement houses, are well known and well regarded and often are managed in a very sophisticated and highly technical fashion; they also have the opportunity to orchestrate and recruit people to engage in socially useful activities. State, local and national governments currently subsidize many Third Sector operations which are generally very labor intensive. One could envision that practice carried further, paying people who "volunteer" for various tasks. With increasing national wealth, these organizations could be involved in creating relatively well-paying jobs in the in-person server category.

An important point often overlooked in many discussions of work is made by Hazel Henderson, who stresses that in an industrial society, the monetized sectors of the economy (including private sector production, public sector infrastructure and the cash-based "underground" economy) are, in a sense, subsidized by the non-monetized social sector as well as by many poorly compensated but indispensable jobs considered "less productive"; e.g., those of school teachers, garbage collectors, cleaners and janitors, mass transit, and road maintenance workers, and others in public service—hospital orderlies, domestics, etc. One of the greatest subsidies to the economy is the unpaid labor of housewives maintain the home and backyard, parent the children, volunteer for a host of community services, and upon whose efforts the whole family's lifestyle depends. This subsidy alone is now estimated world-wide as an uncounted additional average of some 30 percent of GNP.[4]

In the U.S., where more and more families depend on the paychecks of spouses to maintain their desired lifestyles, many of these formerly unpaid jobs are being monetized, as day care centers spring up to take charge of the children, after school learning centers help in the parenting, housecleaning, and lawn care services are provided. Many of these services are poorly paid and are often provided by illegal immigrants who cannot obtain proper compensation under minimum-wage laws. There is no intrinsic, philosophical reason why this work, so necessary to society, cannot be better compensated through increases in the minimum wage and other measures.

In addition to the jobs mentioned above, a number of futurists are predicting an explosion in the demand for workers in the field of elder care. With increases in the older population in the U.S. and elsewhere brought about by advances in medical science there will undoubtedly be a greater demand for in-person services of every sort for this segment of society. Not all jobs in this area will be in the wheel chair pushing category. The technological advances in medical sciences also require a greater degree of skill in administering care including the ability to operate complicated medical equipment, and therefore, caregivers can command higher salaries. The same can be said of many other jobs in the fields of child care and health care in general, as attested by the growth of such professions as nurse practitioners and physician's assistants. Another growth area for jobs is in the fields of leisure and recreation services, including tourism, ranging widely from personal assistants to do shopping and other daily chores to the staff of resorts, theme parks, etc. These jobs, if done with skill and creativity, need not be poorly paid.

Another area that has a great potential for job creation is the whole field of improvement of quality of life, through clean-up and preservation of natural habitats, beautification of public spaces, etc. Indeed, a case can be made that human needs and, hence, the demand for jobs to fulfill these needs is virtually unlimited. Humanistic psychologist, Abraham Maslow, has developed a concept of the hierarchy of human motives, beginning with the most basic (hunger, thirst, sex, sleep, etc.) to safety needs (shelter, protection from danger, etc.) to self-esteem needs (self-confidence, achievement, status, respect, etc.). Once these basic needs are satisfied, the individual is free to pursue the satisfaction of "growth" or "meta" needs, which involve self-actualization, self-development activities, creative acts, altruistic and charitable activities and, in general, realizing one's potential.[5] Some persons consider that with increases in wealth and leisure in the U.S. a growing number of individuals will engage in self-actualization, thus generating demands for goods and, more importantly, for services that hardly exist at the present time, but which could be developed to meet the insatiable demand of persons attempting to realize their fullest human potential. In fact, it can be contended that the fundamental problem of joblessness is not rooted in the demand for workers but in the mismatch between potential jobs and the education and training of job seekers and their availability at the places where jobs are being generated. But, more fundamentally, the question often boils down to a lack of funds and adequate programs to bridge these gaps.

Another creative thinker in this area of new forms of work is David Macarov, who proposes planning for permanent unemployment. In his opinion the search for full employment represents a societal delusion, and given that the world does not need and cannot use all of the human labor available—and as time goes on, will need less and less—he proposes a new social paradigm which does not posit work as its underlying and overreaching value. He suggests, among other things, that the time has come to seriously contemplate the adoption of a universal basic income, regardless of one's activities.[6] Whether his proposal for a scheme involving retirement that can begin at birth is viable at any time in the future or even desirable, given the strong bias in most societies towards considering work as not only an economic but also a moral and psychological necessity, is outside the scope of this book. Nonetheless, I agree with Moravic that working out the details and the societal implications of such a scheme—given the growing numbers of the permanently unemployed—is an effort that should be undertaken.

This question is not only one of social justice. Joseph Coates has pointed out that the core goal of such remedies to massive technological unemployment should be putting a fair share of the gains in productivity into the pockets and purses of everyone in order to keep the machinery of the market economy both working and providing a better life for all. Remedies of this nature should not be viewed solely as income redistribution, "soak the rich" schemes, but as mechanisms to further stimulate the global market economy.

Finally, no discussion of the future of work in the U.S. would be complete without a few words on the future of labor unions and other workers' organizations. Numerous books and articles have been written about this question since, clearly, the power of organized labor has diminished: once representing one third of all workers, unions now represent about one-tenth of them. Experts have a number of suggestions for remedying this situation, including the following:

- To increase union and management cooperation and participation in strategic decisions (.e.g. capital investment, technological change and product mix.

- For unions to act as consultants to management in creating high-performance work systems and push productivity.

- To reformulate labor laws to facilitate productive bargaining relationships through which workplace innovations can emerge.

- To devise collective bargaining provisions which seek to provide affected workers access to and training for the remaining jobs created by the introduction of new technologies.

- To shift the focus of collective bargaining negotiations from the outcome of technological change to the process of change itself, including retraining for displaced workers, skill upgrading, etc.

- To foster research into skill-based alternatives to current technology.

The above suggestions are only a sample of the many solutions being proposed to ease the plight of organized labor, as more and more companies move their plants to localities hostile to unions and replace workers with automated machines, or more whole factories overseas to low-wage countries. In my view, the handwriting is on the wall: the day of the old-style industrial union with its focus on collective bargaining in defining work rules and pay scales is fast coming to an end. This does not, however, signify that the need for workers to band together to foster their own, versus management's interests disappears. The problem is even more acute as the percentage of workers in traditional manufacturing jobs is likely to continue to decline, perhaps eventually to no more than 10 to 15% of the work force. As was pointed out earlier, this reduction in the workforce has already occurred in the agricultural sector; from 75% of workers in 1800, the percentage of farm workers fell to 40% by 1900 and is now in the range of 3% of the workforce. Once again, a full discussion of this topic exceeds the scope of this book, but one approach to the problem looks quite promising. In Charles Heckscher's comprehensive analysis of the current crisis in the U.S. labor relations framework, he argues for "associational unionism", a model outside the tradition of American labor law and practices. Heckscher defines an associational union as an open, professional association with a willingness to pressure employers but, unlike such groups as lawyers' and doctors' associations—this type of organization is open to all workers, office and blue collar employees alike. Heckscher explains that professional associations have a key characteristic workers need now—they are not tied to any job or employee.

> Given the rapid change in the economy and the structure of almost every industry, and the growth of temporary and contingent work, any organization that is built around a stable contract is in trouble. Professions define them-

selves by a sense of shared identity among their members separate from their particular jobs.[7]

The author goes on to explain that professional groups have gone far in helping their members by providing support and services: they provide job placement and advice, skill development, and perhaps most important, portable benefits such as retirement plans and access to health care. They are beginning to learn how to apply pressure to employers using measures that are often far more effective than the strike, such as the creative use of information as a weapon (e.g., publishing lists of the best and worst employers in an industry), offering legal support for members' suits against employers, etc. This brief description can offer only a hint of the detailed and closely argued analysis Heckscher provides of a new system of representation that encourages multilateral negotiation involving management, different groups of employees, and other interested parties. As a person who recently helped a professional association to successfully bring pressure on the management of a major international organization, I can attest to the validity and appeal of many of the concepts Heckscher develops in this visionary work.

In this and previous chapters I have discussed the plight of workers and their unions who fall outside the charmed circle of symbolic analysts and other Information Age workers. I have also mentioned, especially in Chapter 2, some of the remedies that have been suggested for those who cannot easily adjust to the demands of the global economy. At this juncture, it is customary for the book's author to suggest his or her own solutions to the issues raised. I shall refrain from doing so. What I shall do is offer some hope that with growing material wealth we can attempt to solve some of these problems in a way that diminishes the growing pains of adjusting to the new requirements of Information Age living. To attain this additional wealth, any discussions of new economic policies should be centered on methods of stimulating productivity and innovation as a first priority, and then, as hoped for increases in natural wealth begin to materialize, priorities can shift to addressing the need for additional social programs.

The next and final chapter will expand such a positive vision of the future and its relationship to the concept that lies at the heart of this book: the future of the American Dream.

Chapter 8

Beyond the American Dream

The American dream has been defined by one writer not only as the right of all Americans to get rich, but rather their right to have a reasonable chance to achieve "success" material or otherwise, as they define it—through their own efforts, and to attain fulfillment through success.[1]

In this writer's view, "the American Dream" can best be defined by several beliefs which have deep roots in American history. The first two predate the founding of the United States of America; the latter two were developed to the fullest extent during the post-Civil War period, when the U.S. began to industrialize and receive the huge flow of immigrants necessary to work in the fields and factories during this era of intense growth.

(a) *The Belief in Abundance*

David Potter, in People of Plenty, discusses this theme at great length in the context of North American culture.[2] In reality, this vision of the Americas was started by the Spanish explorers and conquistadores in the 16th century (read Columbus's glowing accounts of the fertile lands and rich mineral deposits of the Indies). However, the colonists of North America extended this belief to encompass the expanding frontier as a never-ending supply of unappropriated wealth which, in turn, would bring about a constant supply of economic opportunities. When the continent was occupied by the immigrant hordes, a new variant of the belief arose, one that is still alive today: the explosive growth of scientific and technological knowledge as a never-ending source of plenty. As Christopher Lasch states: "Those who believed in progress were impressed by the technological conquest of scarcity and the collective control over nature that seemed to be inherent in the productive machinery of modern societies. Abundance, they believed, would eventually give everyone access to leisure, cultivation, refinement — advantages formerly restricted to the wealthy."[3]

(b) *The Belief in Progress*

This set of ideas can be traced back to the French and English philosophers of the 18th century during the Age of Enlightenment. It can be argued that such concepts began in pre-modern times, notably in St. Augustine's arguments against the cyclical theories of pagan philosophers. Certainly the roots of these ideas in the U.S. have a venerable lineage, going back to the Founding Fathers of the Republic: the writings of Jefferson, Franklin and others. However, these were not Utopian ideals, as Lasch states: "The idea of progress never rested on the promise of an ideal society... the modern conception of history has no foreseeable conclusion... A social order founded on science...seems to have achieved a kind of immortality undreamed of by earlier civilizations."[4] This vision of the future postulated a general and continued rise in living standards and a population ever more humane, more pacific and more concerned with social justice.

(c) *The Belief in Equality (The "Horatio Alger" Story)*

This set of beliefs is somewhat complex, and yet it lies at the heart of the American Dream. In one formulation, it states that American society offers equality of opportunity, assuming that all citizens are equal under the law and no one is restricted to a station in life by economic status or birth. The liberty and equality protected by the Constitution offer everyone the freedom to grasp the opportunities generated by the country's abundance and progress. The entire American population is in contact with the sources of wealth and hence, "the rising tide raises all boats." Thus, those like Horatio Alger who play by the rules and work hard will, with a little pluck and luck, be winners in American society. Conversely, those who enjoy low status must somehow be responsible for their failures. The important thing is to maintain a "level playing field" (equality of opportunity) so that all who truly want to can succeed. However, as Herbert

Gans points out: "...that conception is also resolutely individualistic, since people are prepared to remove unfair obstacles to opportunity that stand in the way of individuals, but are less willing to help entire groups or classes held back by unfair obstacles."[5] In this same vein, another social scientist comments: "American culture is allergic to the idea that impersonal forces control individual destiny. Rather, we prefer to think of our lives as products of our own efforts. Through hard work, innate ability, and competition, the good prosper and the weak drop by the wayside."[6]

Thus, a note of Social Darwinism enters the belief in equality (this was much emphasized in the later 19th century). We believe that those who are well-equipped to compete will reap the material rewards and those who cannot "cut the mustard" will suffer deprivation.

Another formulation of this belief is that Americans are a resourceful people. If there are obstacles in the way of prosperity, we will clear them away. As one writer puts it, economic catastrophes may wreak destruction across the land, "..but being the pragmatic, can-do people that we are, we pick up the pieces and rebuild our lives in a bigger and better fashion than before. This is the best our culture seems to offer about the problem of economic decline: that it is a temporary problem, and we will overcome it."[7]

(d) *The Belief in Mobility*

As David Potter states: "Americans are conditioned to a habit of constant adjustment, constant adaptation to new circumstances and constant readiness to accept or experiment with what is new."[8] This is the frontier mentality, that practical, inventive turn of mind, quick to find expedients and thus reinforcing the aptitude for exploiting new potentialities in the economy. This habit of mind leads to a willingness of families to relocate in search of better jobs and has spurred the growth of suburbia; as Gans says, "The decentralizing trend is now new, for Americans have headed for the latest frontier since the 17th century... the major contemporary change is that more people and the companies that employ them can afford to be footloose and head for the open spaces farther from the cities… the new growth takes place at the edges of organized society, enabling the people who want the decentralized life to obtain it."[9]

In addition to the above comments on the historical background of the American Dream, it is worth noting that in more recent times, the Dream was shaped by the post-World War II experience. The United States emerged from the war as a global superpower, with the strongest economy on earth. The pent-up demand for goods and services, generated by the Great Depression followed by war, fueled a massive expansion of civilian production which could be accommodated in the new factories built for war production. The U.S. government, following Keynesian economic theories, further spurred economic growth and provided subsidies of various sorts to stimulate housing and infrastructure construction, college education and other benefits for the returning veterans. All this triggered economic and social development in this country that was and is unprecedented. From these good times, which lasted until the oil crisis of the 1970s, grew a series of beliefs that might be classified as the post-war American Dream, and can be summarized as follows:

(a) *The Job*

The expectations for men (and subsequently women, as the feminist movement took hold in the 1960s) is described by Herbert Gans as: "…work that gave them a feeling of importance and accomplishment…with a chance for advancement… for high income, …jobs with no danger of being fired."[10] To this must be added the expectation that one would join a firm and remain there throughout one's working life, and upon retirement, receive a nice pension and other benefits, including social security payments. One key element, in addition to the economic security that the above presupposes, was the expectation of continuing career growth into the upper ranks of management for professionals and to high-paying supervisory jobs (white collar) for blue-collar workers. According to Kathleen Newman the formula for success was clear: "You drove yourself in school, got into a respectable college, picked a practical career, and pushed ahead with your nose at the grindstone. At the end of this long march lay the accoutrements of the good life."[11]

(b) *The House and Car*

Central to the American Dream are the two major material investments the average family makes: the single-family home and car. These acquisitions have a lot of psychological significance: the house maximizes privacy, control over the immediate environment, and as much distance as possible from the next owner. For many middle-class and working-class families after World War II these houses, located primarily in newly-constructed suburbs, represented on one hand an escape from the urban ghetto their parents inhabited, and on the other, the belief — as Newman would have it — that the suburban town "... was supposed to be a place where 'real' Americans — descendents of immigrant stock, children of Depression survivors — could keep the extended family together by moving around the corner."[12] Another concomitant to home ownership was the observation that after purchase, the home tended to appreciate in the real estate market, far in excess of inflation, so that one's home equity value could serve as an added source of financial security in the retirement years.

(c) *Of Rising Living Standards*

This set of expectations includes both economic and social aspects and adds a shining luster to the American Dream, as it breeds great expectations that each successive generation of Americans will live better than their parents in a never-ending upward spiral provided by the increasing abundance to be produced by the economic system. As Potter states: "The economic potentialities of our continent have caused us to subordinate other values to the maximization of wealth, that in the process, we have committed ourselves to an impossible ideal — the ideal of mobility for everyone — with the consequence of causing tensions and insecurities for the individual..."[13] This dream of upward mobility is best expressed by Katherine Newman: "It is an article of faith among middle-class Americans that every generation will do better than the one that preceded it, and that upward mobility is the birthright for those who work hard. By the same token, nothing is due those who slack off and expect a handout."[14]   Elsewhere Newman notes that: "The security of these years of economic expansion allowed a generation with a Depression mentality to heave a sigh of relief. Yet it was sup-posed to be just the beginning. Young-marrieds who came to the suburbs in the 1950s and 1960s — often as the first home-owners in their families — had to do more than simply achieve middle-class life for themselves. They were the shock troops, the front line warriors in their extended family's quest for up-ward mobility."[15]   Finally, this belief in the inevitability of up-ward mobility (provided, or course, that one followed the rules of the game) extended to the next generation, the so-called "baby boomers", born in the late fifties and sixties, who took as a baseline of comparison the income and standard of living of their parents as they were growing up and expected not only to equal these standards but to exceed them, both economically and in every other way, including an upward move in class status — something that no previous generation in American history ex-pected to such an extent.

Is the Dream Deferred or Destroyed?

Before I address this important question, it is necessary to note that for one important segment of American society, the American Dream has had little or no meaning. I refer to the Afro-American community, whose problems are clearly docu-mented in Andrew Hacker's Two Nations. What Hacker does not stress, however, is that for a small but significant segment of the black society, the American Dream is alive and well — these are the unionized blue-collar workers an the white-collar profes-sionals who, through hard work and in spite of many obstacles, have made it into the solid middle class in this country. This had a transforming effect on those Afro-American families who have made it out of the ghetto, breaking down racial prejudices and opening opportunities that until the 1960s were largely closed to Black society.

A number of social critics, including Lesch, Newman and other writers cited in earlier chapters of this book have seriously questioned the continuing viability of the American Dream. According to these writers, the set of expectations subsumed in the Dream appear to have been put on hold, or perhaps destroyed forever.

(a) Employment for the baby boomers is not providing lifetime security or inevitable advancement. In many cases, their jobs are not providing sufficient income to provide the same lifestyles that their parents enjoyed at a comparable age. In many cases, the only way for a couple to maintain an acceptable standard of living is for both spouses to work outside the home.

(b) The goal of acquiring a single-family house in a desirable neighborhood is not easy — the prices of such houses have skyrocketed so that many median-income families are hard pressed to own their own dwellings.

(c) The dream of upward mobility seems questionable; many baby boomers find that low-paying entry-level jobs are available, but the prospects of upward movement are not assured. Others may reach the ranks of middle management only to discover a "glass ceiling"; even worse, some reach these ranks only to learn that their company is eliminating middle management in major corporate restructuring along new non-hierarchical lines.

(d) Finally, the expectation of a comfortable, well-financed retirement, with the economic cushion provided by home equity and social security is no longer the sure thing it was in the 1950s and '60s since no one can count on long-term employment with any one enterprise, as was the case in the post-World War II period.

Obviously, the American middle class has entered a time of real uncertainty. The economy (not just the American, but the global economy) has entered a phase of fundamental transformation that the public, their representatives in government, and even the leading experts little understand and seem hopeless to control. As a consequence, some writers paint a dim future for the American Dream, based as it is on the idea of continued progress and growing abundance. I have described the visions of some of these writers in Chapter 5 and will not repeat them at this juncture. Their prescriptions often involve a redefinition of the American Dream in such a way that the great expectations it has created are reduced to a modest scale, perhaps a return to the petit-bourgeois ideals of 19th century populism.

At the same time, there is a very different outlook for the future of the American economy and society in general, as pointed out in previous chapters devoted to the optimists: those who foresee a bright scenario for this country, not just for the middle class but for all Americans; a vision that speaks of renewed growth, increased abundance, and a strengthening of social justice, with enough additional wealth to confront many remaining social problems.

The main arguments for taking a sanguine view of the future of the American economy are set forth elsewhere in this book, and consist, basically, of three elements. First, a belief in the fundamental soundness of the American economy and its predominant place within a growing global economy. Second, a conviction that, with the end of the Cold War, nation-states may be able to devote their energies and resources to peaceful pursuits rather than undertaking enormously expensive and wasteful arms races. Third, and most importantly, an awareness of the enormous potential for increased wealth and productivity implicit in the revolutionary developments in science and technology in the late 20th century. According to this vision of the future of work and wealth in the 21st century, the American Dream is alive and well. Its main elements — progress, equality and social mobility — are still intact, and the components of the Dream — well-paid and satisfying employment, the family home and a rising standard of living — are still possible to achieve for the majority of Americans.

And so we have two basically different visions of the future: one group that has been labeled the "declinists"; the other that might be called "the cornucopians". Is there anything that these seemingly opposing groups of visionaries share in common? I believe it is fair to state that a great many, if not all, the authors cited in this book would agree with the proposition that American society is undergoing a profound and irreversible transformation from the Industrial Age to what has been called the Post Industrial Age, or the Information Age. The profound changes that are taking place in this country are also occurring elsewhere, as the nations of the world are converting to a global economy. And these changes are occurring, not only in the economy but in all aspects of society; not just in the middle class, although this class is the most profoundly affected at present. Observers of the American scene part company in the interpretation of these trends and the long-term prognosis for change: the two groups present very different pictures of the future and there appears to be little chance of reaching a synthesis of opinion between the two camps.

In this writer's opinion, both groups—the declinists and the cornucopians—are in reality observing and reporting on the same phenomenon, much as the fabled blind men observing the elephant: one blind man felt the trunk, another the belly and a third the tail of the elephant, and each came up with an entirely different description of the beast. Could this be what our social observers are seeing in the case of the American scene — a society undergoing wrenching change with old jobs, old customs and old social arrangements being swept away in a wave of creative destruction? If this is the case, what is the true picture of the future? Will there be a new American Dream, or will it be a nightmare of class warfare and devil-take-the hindmost? What will the Dream consist of? (Certainly not the Ozzie and Harriet life of post World War II America, if such a life ever really existed outside of a Hollywood situation comedy.) Our society and economy have changed too much for a return to the not-so-desirable past.

How does one choose between the gloomy and upbeat visions of the future? The answer, obviously, is that there is no objective way of choosing either vision of the future. In the final analysis, no one can foresee with certainty what the future will bring, especially with respect to long-term prospects. Therefore, the ultimate choice between conflicting versions of the future to a large extent involves highly personal, subjective criteria.

It will be no surprise to the reader that I espouse the outlook of the optimists. My life experience leads me in the direction of cautious optimism. I was born in the depths of the Depression era and have experienced much that has transpired since. I have spent almost my entire professional career in economic and social development work in both the private and public sectors. I have been an active futurist for many years and have done postgraduate work in future studies. All these experiences lead me to view the future of this country in a positive light, since I have experienced in this country and abroad the often traumatic but ultimately successful outcome of economic and social change in market-based societies.

Finally, there is one other consideration: it has been my experience in life that often prophecies become self-fulfilling. If one takes a defeatist, negative approach to the possibilities for progress there is little reason to strive for change. All change is risky, but much of human progress is based on risk taking — acting on incomplete or even conflicting information but with a belief in the possibility of ultimate success. The American Dream has always been based on this fundamental belief. Therefore, I urge the readers of this book to consider the possibility of a new Dream forged in American society, in spite of the confusing, worrisome times in which we live. And thus my book ends on a hopeful note, with an appeal to the optimistic nature in each one of us. I cannot guarantee that this hopeful vision will be realized. At no time in the history of this country has there been any certainty that the American experiment, the first true democracy in world experience, would weather the various trials that fate has provided for it. Nonetheless, many generations of citizens and those aspiring to citizenship have carried on in the hope that this Dream for themselves and their families could be achieved. This is the spirit which inspired the men and women who founded and built this country, it is the spirit which should continue to inspire us to pursue a renewed and more inclusive American Dream as we enter the 21st century.

Another main conclusion of this book has to do with the seemingly disparity of views among the various commentators on the future of the American economy: the optimists and the pessimists; the declinists and the cornucopians. They seem to be describing different Americas, yet when viewed from a different perspective these commentators seem to be singing the same tune; a complicated melody, discordant at times, having to do with the fall of the old industrial order and the rise of an information-based economy. Not a dirge but a song of hope for this dynamic country!

NOTES

Chapter 1: Introduction – Visions of the Future of Work

1.   Louis Uchitelle, "The Middle Class: Winning in Politics, Losing in Life", <u>New York Times</u>, 19 July 1998, 4:1.

2.   Peter Schwartz and Peter Leyden, "The Long Boom", <u>Wired</u>, July 1997, 5:7.

3.   <u>See References</u>. At this point, it should be noted that the future time frame of this book is about 30 years out - any speculation of what may transpire after that properly belongs in the realm of science fiction.

4.   Drucker, <u>Post Capitalist Society</u>, 69.

5.   Rifkin, <u>The End of Work</u>, xviii.

6.   Bryan and Farrell, <u>Market Unbound</u>, 10, 20.

7.   Wriston, <u>The Twilight of Sovereignty</u>, 103.

8.   Wriston, 18.

Chapter 2: The Pessimists' Vision

1.   Reich, <u>The Work of Nations</u>, 8-9.

2.   Reich, 48.

3.   Reich, 56.

4.	Reich, 81.

5.	Reich, 104.

6.	Reich, 112.

7.	Reich, 113.

8.	Reich, 132.

9.	See <u>References</u>.

10.	Drucker, 69-70.

11.	Reich, 177.

12.	Rifkin, 110.

13.	Reich, 214.

14.	See <u>References</u>.

15.	Ethan Kapstein, "Workers and the World Economy;" <u>Foreign Affairs</u>, May/June 1996, 22.

16.	Wilson, <u>When Work Disappears</u>, xiii.

17.	Reich, 177.

18.	Kapstein, 16 and 18.

19.	Many of these recommended solutions are contained in "Impact of Changing Employment: If the Good Jobs Go Away", <u>Annals</u>, <u>March 1996</u>, <u>Vol. 544</u>, and Aronowitz and Di Fazio, <u>The Jobless Future</u>.

20.	Kapstein, 27.

21.   Wilson, 233.

Chapter 3: The Optimists' Vision

1.   Zey, <u>Seizing the Future</u>, 17.

2.   Schwartz and Leyden, 115-16.

3.   Schwartz and Leyden, 118.

4.   Toffler, <u>Creating a New Civilization</u>, 19.

5.   Wriston, xi.

6.   Moynihan, <u>Coming American Renaissance</u>, 14-15.

7.   Moynihan, 17.

8.   See <u>AEI Studies on Understanding Economic Inequality</u>.

9.   Wriston, 46.

10.   Gingrich, <u>Window of Opportunity</u>, 19.

11.   Gingrich, 88.

12.   McKenzie, <u>Paradox of Progress</u>, 152-153.

Chapter 4: A New Policy Player: The Global Capital Market

1.   W. Michael Blumenthal, "the World Economy and
        Technological Change", <u>Foreign Affairs</u>, 1988, Vol. 66
        no. 3.

2.   Wriston, 65.

3.   Salomon, Virtual Money, 233.

4.   Wriston, 65-70.

5.   Thomas Friedman, "When Money Talks, Governments Listen", New York Times, 24 July 1994.

6.   There is little chance of reconciling this figure with the $3.2 trillion figure mentioned earlier. The huge high speed turnover of the global market and the fact that few official statistics are kept lead to double counting and other inaccuracies. The true size in the early 1990's of the market is probably somewhere between these two figures. (According to Elena Harris Saloman in Virtual Money, the figure is around $2.2 trillion.)

7.   See footnote 5.

8.   Bryan and Farrell, 120.

9.   Bryan and Farrell, 136.

Chapter 5: America in Decline?

1.   Heilbroner, Visions of the Future, 101.

2.   Heilbroner, 108.

3.   Madrick, End of Affluence, 164.

4.   Madrick, 105.

5.   Greenwood, Third Industrial Revolution, 24.

6.   Samuelson, <u>Good Life and its Discontents</u>, 234-5.

7.   Jeffrey Madrick, "Computers: Waiting for the Revolu-
          tion", <u>New York Review of Books</u>, 26 March 1998.

Chapter 6: New Paradigms of Wealth and Work

1.   Easterlin, <u>Growth Triumphant</u>, 20.

2.   Wriston, 18-19.

3.   Easterlin, 3.

4.   Easterlin, 2.

5.   David A. Patterson, "Microprocessors in 2020", <u>Scien-
          tific American</u>, September 1995.

6.   Gates, <u>Road Ahead</u>, 33.

7.   Schwartz and Leyden, "The Long Boom", 118.

8.   Moynihan, <u>Coming American Renaissance</u>, 112.

9.   Schwartz and Leyden, 168.

10.   Coates, et. al., <u>2025</u>, 3.

11.   G. Pascal Zachary, "Service Productivity is Rising
          Fast...", <u>Wall Street Journal</u>, 8 June 1995.

12.   See <u>References</u>.

13.   Coates et. al., 100-101 and 337-338.

14.   Schwartz and Leyden, 122-127.

Chapter 7: A Time of Great Abundance

1.   Schwartz and Leyden, 116.

2.   Of particular importance are the publications of the U.S. Department of Labor, Bureau of Labor Statistics, especially "Employment Outlook; 1996-2006" and "Career Guide to Industries".

3.   Jeffrey Madrick, "Computers: Waiting for the Revolution", New York Review of Books, 26 March 1998.

4.   Henderson, Paradigms of Progress, 11.

5.   See References.

6.   Macarov, "The Employment of New Ends: Planning for Permanent Employment," Annals, March 1996.

7.   Heckscher, The New Unionism, ix.

Chapter 8: Beyond the American Dream

1.   Hochschild, Facing Up to the American Dream, xvii.

2.   Potter, People of Plenty.

3.   Lasch, The True and Only Heaven, 530-1.

4.   Lasch, 48.

5.   Gans, Middle American Individualism, 37.

6.   Newman, Declining Fortunes, 89.

7.   Newman, 25-6.

8.   Potter, People of Plenty, 157.

9.   Gans, 91.

10.   Gans, 25.

11.   Newman, 1.

12.   Newman, 153.

13.   Potter, 156.

14.   Newman, 139.

15.   Newman, 91.

REFERENCES

American Academy of Political and Social Science. <u>Annals,</u> <u>Vol. 544</u>, Philadelphia, PA: A.B. Shostak, Special Editor, March 1996.

American Enterprise Institute for Public Policy Research. <u>AEI</u> <u>Studies on Understanding Economic Inequality</u>, Washington, D.C.: M.H. Kosters, Series Editor, various dates.

Aranowitz, S. and W. Di Fazio. <u>The Jobless Future</u>. Minneapolis: University of Minnesota Press, 1994.

Blumenthal, W.M. "The Whole Economy and Technological Change." <u>Foreign Affairs</u>, Vol. 66 no. 3 (1988).

Bryan, L. and D. Farrell. <u>Market Unbound</u>. New York: John Wiley & Sons Inc., 1996.

Coates, J.B., J.B. Mahaffie and A. Hines. 2025: <u>Scenarios of</u> <u>U.S. Global Society Reshaped by Science and Technology</u>. Greensboro: Oakhill Press, 1997.

Drucker, P. <u>Managing in a Time of Great Change</u>. New York: Dutton, 1995.

_____, <u>Post Capitalist Society</u>. New York: Harper Business, 1993.

Easterlin, R.A. <u>Growth Triumphant</u>. Ann Arbor: University of Michigan Press, 1996.

Friedman, T.L. "When Money Talks, Governments Listen", <u>New York Times</u> (July 24, 1994).

Gans, H. <u>Middle American Individualism</u>. New York: Oxford University Press, 1988.

Gates, W. <u>The Road Ahead</u>. New York: Viking, 1995.

Gingrich, N. <u>Window of Opportunity</u>. New York: St. Martins Press, 1984.

Grace, E.S. <u>Biotechnology Unzipped</u>. Washington, D.C.: Joseph Henry Press, 1997.

Greenwood, J. "The Third Industrial Revolution" in AEI Studies on Understanding Economic Inequality, ed. M.H. Kosters. Washington, D.C.: AEI, 1997.

Hacker, A. <u>Two Nations: Black and White, Separate, Hostile and Unequal</u>. New York: Scribners, 1992.

Heckscher, C.C. <u>The New Unionism</u>. Ithaca: Cornell University Press, 1988.

Heilbroner, R. <u>Visions of the Future</u>. New York: Oxford University Press, 1995.

Henderson, H. <u>Paradigms of Progress</u>. Indianapolis: Knowledge Systems Inc., 1993.

Hochschild, J.L. <u>Facing Up to the American Dream</u>. Princeton: Princeton University Press, 1995.

Kapstein, E.B. "Workers and the World Economy," <u>Foreign Affairs</u>, (May/June 1996).

Kuhn, T. <u>The Structure of Scientific Revolutions</u>. Chicago: University of Chicago Press, 1996.

Lasch, C. The True and Only Heaven. New York: W.W. Norton & Co., 1991.

Macarov, D. "The Employment of New Ends: Planning for Permanent Employment." Annals (March 1996).

Madrick, J. "Computers: Waiting for the Revolution", New York Review of Books (March 26, 1998).

_____, The Ends of Affluence. New York: Random House, 1995.

Maslow, A.H. Further Reaches of Human Nature. New York: Viking, 1971.

McKenzie, R.B. The Paradox of Progress. New York: Oxford University Press, 1997.

Monyihan, M. The Coming American Renaissance. New York: Simon & Schuster, 1996.

Newman, K. Declining Fortunes. New York: Basic Books, 1993.

Patterson, D.A. "Microprocessors in 2020". Scientific American (September 1995).

Potter, D.M. People of Plenty. Chicago: University of Chicago Press, 1954.

Reich, R.B. The Work of Nations. New York: Vintage Books, 1992.

Rifkin, J. The End of Work. New York: G.P. Putnam & Sons, 1995.

Salomon, E.H. Virtual Money. New York: Oxford University Press, 1997.

Samuelson, R. The Good Life and Its Discontents. New York: Times Books, 1995.

Schwartz, P. and P. Leyden. "The Long Boom". Wired (July 1997).

Toffler, A. The Third Wave. New York: Bantam Books, 1990.

Toffler, A. and H. Toffler. Creating a New Civilization. Atlanta: Turner Publishing Inc., 1994.

Uchitelli, L. "The Middle Class: Winning in Politics, Losing in Life". New York Times (July 19, 1998).

U.S. Department of Labor.
- Employment Outlook, 1996-2006
- Career Guide to Industries
Washington, D.C. Bureau of Labor Statistics

Wilson, W.J. When Work Disappears. New York: Alfred A. Knopf, 1996.

World Future Society
- The Futurist (monthly magazine)
- Future Survey (monthly abstract of books, articles and reports)
- Future Research and Quarterly (scholarly quarterly)
7910 Woodmont Avenue, Bethesda, MD 20897

Winston, W.B. The Twilight of Sovereignty. New York: Charles Scribner's Sons, 1992.

Zachary, G.P. "Service Productivity is Rising Fast" Wall Street Journal (June 8, 1995)

Zey, M.G. Seizing the Future. New York: Simon & Schuster, 1994.

Zuboff, S. In the Age of Smart Machine. New York: Basic Books, 1988.

About the Author

Thomas Carson has been in the field of international banking and economic and social development for over 30 years and with future studies for over 15 years, both as a Professional Member of The World Future Society and Guest Lecturer at several university business schools as well as recently completing future-oriented studies at the graduate level at a major university. He has published articles on future-related subjects and has spoken to numerous groups both here and in Latin America. The author would greatly appreciate your comments on this book which can be sent by e-mail to the following address:

Tcarson@mailcity.com

www.ingramcontent.com/pod-product-compliance
Lightning Source LLC
Chambersburg PA
CBHW020542290526
45786CB00002B/998

* 9 7 8 1 5 8 5 0 0 1 1 3 2 *